# Air Fryer

# Cookbook

## For Beginners

**120 Simple Recipes for Beginners and Advanced Users to Fry, Grill, Roast, and Bake Tasty Homemade Meals.**

John B. McGowan

# TABLE OF CONTENTS

# INTRODUCTION

Are you constantly on the lookout for more convenient and up-to-date methods of preparing the best meals for you and your family?

Are you continuously on the lookout for beneficial kitchen tools that will make your time spent in the kitchen a little more enjoyable?

After all, you won't have to look any further now! We are pleased to introduce to you today the best kitchen gadget currently available on the market: the air fryer!

For a variety of reasons, air fryers are the best kitchen appliances available.

Are you interested in learning more about air fryers? If so, keep reading. After that, pay attention!

First and foremost, you should be aware that air fryers are unique and revolutionary kitchen appliances that cook your food by circulating hot air around it. These tolls make use of a special technology known as rapid air technology to operate. Therefore, all of the food cooked in these fryers is succulent on the inside while being perfectly cooked on the outside, resulting in a delicious meal.

You should also know that air fryers can be used to cook, bake, steam, and roast just about anything you can think of, which is the next thing you should know.

In conclusion, you should be aware that air fryers allow you to cook your meals in a much healthier manner.

A large number of people all over the world have fallen in love with this wonderful and amazing tool, and it is now your turn to become one of those people.

Consequently, we strongly advise you to acquire an air fryer immediately and to get your hands on this cooking journal as soon as you possibly can!

You'll learn how to cook the best breakfasts, lunches, side dishes, snacks and appetizers, fish and seafood recipes, meat and poultry recipes, and vegetable recipes, as well as the best desserts, with your new kitchen gadget in this recipe collection.

We can assure you that all of the meals you prepare in your air fryer will be delicious and that everyone will be impressed by your culinary abilities from the moment you start using it! So let's get this party started!

Enjoy your time in the kitchen with your fantastic air fryer!

# AIR FRYER BREAKFAST RECIPES

# TASTY BAKED EGGS

**Preparation time:** 10 minutes **Cooking time:** 20 minutes **Servings:** 4

## Ingredients:

- 4 quail eggs
- 2 cups baby spinach, chopped into bite-size pieces7 ounces of ham, diced, 4 tablespoons of milk
- 1 tbsp olive oil (extra virgin)1 tablespoon nonstick cooking spray
- Season with salt and black pepper to taste.

## Directions:

1. Formalized paraphrase Heat a skillet with the oil over medium heat until hot, then add the baby spinach and swirl to cook for a couple of minutes before removing from the heat.
2. Cooking spray should be used to grease four ramekins before dividing the young spinach and ham among them.
3. Pour one egg into each ramekin and divide the milk among them. Season the ramekins liberally with salt and pepper before placing them in an air fryer preheated to 350°F and baking for 20 minutes.
4. Baked eggs can be served for breakfast. Enjoy!

The following are the nutritional values: calories 321, fat 6, fiber 8, carbohydrates 15, protein 12.

# BREAKFAST EGG BOWLS

**Preparation time:** 10 minutes **Cooking time:** 20 minutes **Servings:** 4

## Ingredients:

- 4 dinner rolls, with the tops removed and the insides scooped out. 4 tablespoons of heavy cream (optional)
- 4 quail eggs
- 4 tablespoons of chives and parsley combined, seasoned with salt and black pepper to taste.
- 4 tbsp parmesan cheese, grated

## Directions:

1. Place the dinner rolls on a baking sheet and crack an egg into each one.
2. Bake for 20 minutes at 350°F.
3. To assemble each roll, divide heavy cream and mixed herbs among them, seasoning with salt and pepper.
4. Cook the rolls for 20 minutes at 350 degrees F in the air fryer after sprinkling them with parmesan cheese. 3.
5. Arrange your bread bowls on plates and serve them for breakfast the next morning. Enjoy!

238 calories; 4 grams of fat; 7 grams of fiber; 14 grams of carbohydrates; and 7 grams of protein

# DELICIOUS BREAKFAST SOUFFLÉ

**Preparation time:** 10 minutes **Cooking time:** 8 minutes **Servings:** 4

## Ingredients:

- Four eggs, lightly whisked
- 4 tablespoons of heavy cream (optional)
- A pinch of ground red chili pepper (preferably smashed). 2 teaspoons parsley, finely chopped
- 2 tablespoons of chives, finely chopped, salt and freshly ground black pepper to taste.

## Directions:

1. In a large mixing basin, whisk together the eggs, salt, pepper, heavy cream, red chili pepper, parsley, and chives until well combined, then distribute among four soufflé dishes.
2. Arrange the plates in the air fryer and cook the soufflés for 8 minutes at 350°F.
3. Make sure they're hot when you serve them. Enjoy!

Nutritional information 300 calories, 7 grams of fat, 9 grams of fiber, 15 grams of carbohydrates, and 6 grams of protein.

# AIR FRIED SANDWICH

**Preparation time:** 10 minutes **Cooking time:** 6 minutes **Servings:** 2

## Ingredients:

- 2 English muffins with melted butter
- 2 strips of bacon.
- Season with salt and black pepper to taste.

## Directions:

1. Crack eggs into your air fryer and place them on top of the bacon. Cook for 6 minutes, covered, at 392°F.
2. Microwave the English muffin halves for a few seconds, then split the eggs between the two halves, top with bacon and season with salt and pepper before covering with the other two English muffin halves and serving for breakfast.
3. Enjoy!

The following are the nutritional values: calories 261, fat 5, fiber 8, carbohydrates 12, protein 4.

# RUSTIC BREAKFAST

**Preparation time:** 10 minutes **Cooking time:** 13 minutes **Servings:** 4

## Ingredients:

- 7 oz. of baby spinach8 halved chestnut mushrooms, Eight halved tomatoes 1 minced garlic clove4 chipolatas 7 oz. of baby spinach
- 4 bacon pieces, sliced and diced.
- Season with salt and black pepper to taste. 4 quail eggs
- Using cooking spray

## Directions:

1. Heat the oil in a large skillet over medium heat, then add the tomatoes, garlic, and mushrooms.
2. Toss in the bacon and chipolatas, as well as the spinach and the eggs at the end.
3. Season with salt and pepper, then place the pan in the air fryer's cooking basket and cook at 350°F for 13 minutes, stirring halfway through.
4. Distribute the mixture among the plates and serve it for breakfast. Enjoy!

Nutritional values: 312 calories, 6 grams of fat, 8 grams of fiber, 15 grams of carbohydrates, and 5 grams of protein.

# EGG MUFFINS

**Preparation time:** 10 minutes **Cooking time:** 15 minutes **Servings:** 4

## Ingredients:

- 1 egg
- 2 tbsp olive oil (extra-virgin)3 tblsp. of whole milk.
- 1 cup (3.5 oz.) white flour
- 1 tablespoon of baking powder (optional). 2 oz. grated parmesan cheese
- A dash of Worcestershire sauce is a nice touch.

## Directions:

1. In a large mixing basin, whisk together the eggs, flour, oil, baking powder, milk, Worcestershire sauce, and parmesan cheese until thoroughly combined. Divide the batter among four silicon muffin cups.
2. 2Using your air fryer's cooking basket, arrange the cups in a circular pattern and cook at 392 degrees F for 15 minutes.
3. Serve while it's still warm for breakfast. Enjoy!

The following are the nutritional values: calories 251, fat 6, fiber 8, carbohydrates 9, protein 3.

# POLENTA BITES

**Preparation time:** 10 minutes **Cooking time:** 20 minutes **Servings:** 4

## Ingredients:

For the polenta, follow these instructions:

- 1 tablespoon of melted butter.
- 1 cup cornmeal, ground
- 3 quarts of water.
- Season with salt and black pepper to taste.
- For the polenta bits, prepare the following:
- Powdered sugar (about 2 teaspoons) Cooking spray

## Directions:

1. In a large saucepan, combine the water, cornmeal, butter, salt, and pepper, stirring constantly. Bring to a boil over medium heat, cook for 10 minutes, then remove from heat, whisk once more, and chill until cold.
2. Scoop You only need one spoonful of polenta shaped into a ball and placed on a work surface!
3. -Repeat the process with the remaining polenta balls, placing them all in the cooking basket of your air fryer and spraying them with cooking spray before covering and cooking for 8 minutes at 380 degrees F.
4. Spread sugar on each plate and serve the polenta bits as a breakfast option.
5. Enjoy!

The following are the nutritional values: calories 231, fat 7, fiber 8, carbohydrates 12, protein 4.

# DELICIOUS BREAKFAST POTATOES

**Preparation time:** 10 minutes **Cooking time:** 35 minutes **Servings:** 4

## Ingredients:

- 2 tbsp olive oil (extra-virgin)Cubed potatoes 1 chopped yellow onion, 1 chopped red bell pepper3 potatoes From Fluency
- Season with salt and black pepper to taste. Optional: 1 teaspoon garlic powder
- 1 teaspoon of paprika (sweet) Optional: 1 teaspoon onion powder

## Directions:

1. Toss potatoes with olive oil in an air fryer basket that has been greased with olive oil. Season with salt and pepper to taste.
2. Toss in the onion, bell pepper, garlic powder, paprika, and onion powder, and simmer at 370 degrees F for 30 minutes, or until the vegetables are tender.
3. Divide the potato mixture among the plates and serve it as a breakfast dish. Enjoy!

Nutritional information 214 calories, 6 grams of fat, 8 grams of fiber, 15 grams of carbohydrates, and 4 grams of protein.

# TASTY CINNAMON TOAST

**Preparation time:** 10 minutes **Cooking time:** 5 minutes **Servings:** 6

## *Ingredients:*

- 1 stick of unsalted butter, 12 slices of sourdough bread
- 1 pound sugar
- 1 and 1/2 teaspoons pure vanilla extract
- 1 and 1/2 teaspoons ground cinnamon powder

**Directions:**

1. Formalized paraphraseIn a large mixing basin, beat together soft butter, sugar, vanilla, and cinnamon until thoroughly combined.
2. Spread the mixture over the bread slices and bake at 400 degrees F for 5 minutes, or until golden brown.
3. Divide the mixture evenly between the plates and serve for breakfast. Enjoy!

The following are the nutritional values: calories 221, fat 4, fiber, 7, carbohydrates 12, protein 8.

# DELICIOUS POTATO HASH

**Preparation time:** 10 minutes **Cooking time:** 25 minutes **Servings:** 4

## Ingredients:

- 1 and a half potatoes, cubed.
- 1 chopped yellow onion 2 teaspoons olive oil1 and a half potatoes, cubed.
- 1 chopped green bell pepperSalt and black pepper to taste 1 chopped green bell pepper
- One-and-a-half teaspoons of dried thyme

## Directions:

1. After adding oil and heating it up, cook for 5 minutes at 350 degrees F in your air fryer.2. Cook for another 5 minutes after adding the onion, bell pepper, salt, and pepper.
2. Stir in the potatoes, thyme, and eggs until well combined, then cover and bake for 20 minutes at 360°F.
3. Divide the mixture evenly between the plates and serve for breakfast.Enjoy!

The following are the nutritional values: calories 241, fat 4, fiber 7, carbohydrates 12, protein 7.

# SWEET BREAKFAST CASSEROLE

**Preparation time:** 10 minutes **Cooking time:** 30 minutes **Servings:** 4

## Ingredients:

- 3 tablespoons of brown sugar (optional). 4 tablespoons of melted butter
- 2 teaspoons of refined white sugar.
- 1 to 1/2 teaspoons cinnamon powder
- 1 pound of flour
- To make the dish, use the following ingredients:
- Two quail eggs
- 2 teaspoons of refined white sugar. 2 and a half cups of all-purpose flour. 1 teaspoon (optional) baking soda
- 1 tsp baking powder (optional)2 quail eggs
- 1/2 cup of milk
- two quarts buttermilk
- 4 tablespoons of melted butter
- 1 lemon's zest, grated, and 2/3 cup of blueberries are all you need.

## Directions:

1. In a large mixing bowl, whisk together the eggs, 2 tablespoons white sugar, 2 to 12 cups white flour, baking powder, baking soda, 2 eggs, milk, buttermilk, 4 tablespoons butter, lemon zest, and blueberries. Pour the batter into a pan that will fit your air fryer and bake for 30 minutes at 350 degrees.
2. To make the crumble: In another basin, combine 3 tablespoons of brown sugar with 2 tablespoons of white sugar, 4 tablespoons of butter, 1/2 cups of flour, and cinnamon, stirring until well combined; spread on top of the blueberry mixture.

3. Place in a preheated air fryer and bake at 300 degrees F for 30 minutes.
4. Distribute the mixture among the plates and serve it for breakfast. Enjoy!

Nutritional information 214 calories, 5 grams of fat, 8 grams of fiber, 12 grams of carbohydrates, and 5 grams of protein.

# EGGS CASSEROLE

**Preparation time:** 10 minutes **Cooking time:** 25 minutes **Servings:** 6

## Ingredients:

- 1 pound ground turkey, preferably with 1 tablespoon extra-virgin olive oil
- 1/2 tablespoon chili powder12 hens' eggs
- 1 medium-sized diced sweet potato 1 cup baby spinach (optional)
- Season with salt and black pepper to taste. 2 tomatoes, peeled and diced for serving.

## Directions:

1. In a large mixing bowl, whisk together the eggs, salt, pepper, chili powder, potato, spinach, turkey, and sweet potato until thoroughly combined.
2. Preheat your air fryer to 350°F, then add the oil and heat it through.
3. Pour in the egg mixture and spread it out in your air fryer. Cover it and cook it for 25 minutes.
4. Distribute the mixture among the plates and serve it for breakfast. Enjoy!

Nutritional information 300 calories, 5 grams of fat, 8 grams of fiber, 13 grams of carbohydrates, and 6 grams of protein.

# SAUSAGE, EGGS AND CHEESE MIX

**Preparation time:** 10 minutes **Cooking time:** 20 minutes **Servings:** 4

## Ingredients:

- 10 ounces of cooked and shredded sausage.
- 6 tablespoons melted butter1 cup shredded cheddar cheese 2 cups shredded mozzarella cheese 8 eggs
- 1 cup of milk was whisked
- Season with salt and black pepper to taste. Using cooking spray

## Directions:

1. Toss the sausages with the cheese and mozzarella in a large mixing dish until well combined. 2., 3., 4., 5., 6., 7., and 9.
2. Preheat your air fryer to 380°F and spray with cooking spray before adding the eggs and sausage mixture and cooking for 20 minutes.
3. Distribute the mixture among the plates and serve. Enjoy!

Nutritional information: 320 calories, 6 grams of fat, 8 grams of fiber, 12 grams of carbohydrates, and 5 grams of protein.

# CHEESE AIR FRIED BAKE

**Preparation time:** 10 minutes **Cooking time:** 20 minutes **Servings:** 4

## Ingredients:

- 4 bacon pieces, fried until crispy and crumbled. 2 quarts of milk.
- Two eggs, two and a half cups of cheddar cheese, and one pound of breakfast sausage, casings removed, and shredded.
- 1/2 tsp onions powder
- Season with salt and black pepper to taste. 3 tablespoons of parsley, finely chopped. Cooking oil should be sprayed on

## Directions:

1. In a large mixing bowl, whisk together the eggs, milk, cheese, onion powder, salt, pepper, and parsley until thoroughly combined.
2. Spray the inside of your air fryer with cooking spray and preheat to 320°F before adding the bacon and sausage.
3. Pour in the egg mixture. Smooth it out. Bake for 20 minutes.
4. Distribute the mixture among the plates and serve it. Enjoy!

214 calories, 5 grams of fat, 8 grams of fiber, 12 grams of carbohydrates, and 12 grams of protein.

# BISCUITS CASSEROLE

**Preparation time:** 10 minutes **Cooking time:** 15 minutes **Servings:** 8

## Ingredients:

- 12 ounces of biscuits, cut into fourths, 3 tablespoons of flour
- 1/2 pound chopped sausage
- a pinch of salt and freshly ground black peppertwo and a half gallons milk
- Using cooking spray

## Directions:

1. Spray the inside of your air fryer with cooking spray and preheat it to over 350°F.
2. Spread biscuits on the bottom of the pan and top with meat.
3. In a medium-sized mixing bowl, whisk together the flour, milk, salt, and pepper. Set aside. 2.
4. Distribute the mixture among the plates and serve it for breakfast. Enjoy!

The following are the nutritional values: calories 321, fat 4, fiber 7, carbohydrates 12, protein 5.

# TURKEY BURRITO

**Preparation time:** 10 minutes **Cooking time:** 10 minutes **Servings:** 2

## Ingredients:

- 4 slices of turkey breast that have already been cooked.
- 1/2 sliced red bell peppers 2 eggs
- peeled and pitted. 1 small avocado (cut into slices). salsa (about 2 teaspoons)
- Season with salt and black pepper to taste. 1/8 cup mozzarella cheese, with shredded tortillas on the side

## Directions:

1. In a large mixing bowl, whisk together the eggs and season with salt and pepper to taste. Pour the mixture into a pan and place it in the air fryer basket.
2. Cook for 5 minutes at 400°F before removing the pan from the fryer and transferring the eggs to a serving plate.
3. Arrange the tortillas on a work surface and divide the eggs among them, as well as the turkey meat, bell pepper, cheese, salsa, and avocado among them.
4. After you've prepared your air fryer with tin foil, roll your burritos and place them in the air fryer to cook.
5. Bake the burritos for 3 minutes at 300°F, then divide them among plates and serve.
6. Enjoy!

Nutritional information: 349 calories, 23 grams of fat, 11 grams of fiber, 20 grams of carbohydrates, and 21 grams of protein.

# TOFU SCRAMBLE

**Preparation time:** 5 minutes **Cooking time:** 30 minutes **Servings:** 4

Ingredients:

- Ingredients: 1 brick of tofu, cubed
- 1 teaspoon turmeric, freshly ground
- Another 2 tblsp. of extra virgin olive oil 4 cups of broccoli florets (optional)
- 1/2 tsp onions powder
- 1/2 tsp. garlic powder
- 2 and a 1/2-cup red potato, cut into cubes.
- 1/2 cup chopped yellow onion, salt and black pepper to taste

**Directions:**

1. In a large mixing bowl, combine the tofu, 1 tablespoon oil, salt, pepper, soy sauce, garlic powder, onion powder, turmeric, and onion. Set aside after thoroughly mixing.
2. Combine the potatoes with the remaining oil and seasonings (salt and pepper to taste) in a separate bowl and toss well to coat.
3. Preheat your air fryer to 350°F and bake the potatoes for 15 minutes, shaking halfway through.
4. Bake the tofu in the air fryer for 15 minutes at 350 °F with the marinade.
5. Add the broccoli to the fryer and cook for another 5 minutes, or until the broccoli is tender.
6. Put the dish on the table as soon as possible. Enjoy!

140 calories, 4 g of fat, 3 g of fiber, 10 g of carbohydrates, and 14 g of protein

# OATMEAL CASSEROLE

**Preparation time:** 10 minutes **Cooking time:** 20 minutes **Servings:** 8

## Ingredients:

- 2 cups of rolled oats (or equivalent)
- 1 tsp baking powder (optional) third cup of brown sugar
- Optional: 1 tsp cinnamon powder
- 1 pound chocolate chipsA third cup of blueberries
- 1 banana that has been peeled and mashed. 2 quarts of milk.
- 1 egg
- 2 teaspoons of melted butter.
- 1 tsp vanilla extractCooking spray 1 tablespoon of olive oil

### Directions:

1. In a large mixing basin, combine the sugar, baking powder, cinnamon, chocolate chips, blueberries, and banana, stirring constantly.
2. In a separate bowl, whisk together the eggs, vanilla extract, and butter until well combined.
3. Preheat your air fryer to 320°F and spray the inside with cooking spray before adding the oats to the bottom.
4. Stir in the cinnamon-egg mixture and bake for 20 minutes.
5. Stir it one more time, divide it into bowls, and serve it for breakfast the next morning. Enjoy!

Nutritional information 300 calories, 4 grams of fat, 7 grams of fiber, 12 grams of carbohydrates, and 10 grams of protein.

# HAM BREAKFAST

**Preparation time:** 10 minutes **Cooking time:** 15 minutes **Servings:** 6

## Ingredients:

- 6 cups of French bread, cubed
- 4 ounces chopped green chilies 10 ounces cubed ham 4 ounces shredded cheddar cheese 2 cups milk
- 5 eggs
- 1 tablespoon of Dijon mustard.
- Season with salt and black pepper to taste. Using cooking spray

## Directions:

1. Before using your air fryer, preheat it to 350 degrees Fahrenheit and coat it with cooking spray.
2. In a large mixing bowl, whisk together the eggs, milk, cheese, mustard, salt, and pepper.
3. Toss bread cubes with chilies and ham in the air fryer until well combined.
4. Pour in the egg mixture, smooth it out, and bake it for 15 minutes.
5. Distribute the mixture among the plates and serve. Enjoy!

Nutritional information: 200 calories, 5 grams of fat, 6 grams of fiber, 12 grams of carbohydrates, and 14 grams of protein.

# TOMATO AND BACON BREAKFAST

**Preparation time:** 10 minutes **Cooking time:** 30 minutes **Servings:** 6

## Ingredients:

- 1 pound cubed white bread
- 1 pound cooked and chopped smoked bacon
- 1 tablespoon extra virgin olive oil
- 1 finely sliced small yellow onion
- 28 ounces of canned tomatoes, finely minced
- 1 and 12 teaspoons of crushed red pepper flakes.
- 1/2 pound cheddar cheese, shredded
- 2 teaspoons chives, finely chopped
- 1/2 pound of shredded Monterey Jack cheese with 2 teaspoons of chicken broth.
- Season with salt and black pepper to taste. 8 eggs, lightly whisked

## Directions:

1. Prepare your air fryer by filling it halfway with oil and heating it to 350 degrees F.
2. In a large mixing bowl, combine the bread, bacon, onion, tomatoes, red pepper, and stock.
3. Add the eggs, cheddar, and Monterey jack cheeses and continue to cook for another 20 minutes.
4. Divide the mixture among the plates and garnish them with chives before serving. Enjoy!

The following are the nutritional values: calories 231, fat 5, fiber 7, carbohydrates 12, protein 4.

# TASTY HASH

**Preparation time:** 10 minutes **Cooking time:** 15 minutes **Servings:** 6

## Ingredients:

- Hash browns (16 oz.)
- 1 tablespoon extra virgin olive oil
- paprika, 1/2 teaspoon
- 1/2 tsp. garlic powder
- Salt and black pepper to taste. 1 whisked egg
- 2 tablespoons chopped chives 1 cup shredded cheddar

## Directions:

1. Heat the oil in your air fryer to 350 degrees F, then add the hash.
2. Toss in the paprika, garlic powder, salt, pepper, and egg, and cook for 15 minutes.
3. Toss in the cheddar and chives, divide among plates, and serve!

Nutrition: 213 calories, 7 grams of fat, 8 grams of fiber, 12 grams of carbohydrates, and 4 grams of protein.

# BREAKFAST PEA TORTILLA

**Preparation time:** 10 minutes **Cooking time:** 7 minutes **Servings:** 8

## Ingredients:

- A 1/2 pound bag of baby peas
- 4 tablespoons of melted butter 1
- 1/2 cup plain yogurt8 quail eggs
- 1/2 cup mint, chopped
- Season with salt and black pepper to taste.

## Directions:

1. Melt the butter in a pan that fits your air fryer over medium heat, then add the peas and cook for a couple of minutes, stirring constantly.
2. In the meantime, whisk together half of the yogurt with the salt, pepper, eggs, and mint in a large mixing bowl.
3. Cook for 7 minutes at 350 degrees F, after pouring the sauce over the peas and tossing them together. 3.
4. Spread the remaining yogurt over your tortilla, slice it, and serve it immediately. Enjoy!

Nutritional information 192 calories, 5 grams of fat, 4 grams of fiber, 8 grams of carbohydrates, and 7 grams of protein.

# MUSHROOM OATMEAL

**Preparation time:** 10 minutes **Cooking time:** 20 minutes **Servings:** 4

## *Ingredients:*

- 1 cup steel-cut oats, cooked1 finely chopped tiny yellow onion
- minced Two cloves of garlic (or more) 2 tablespoons of butter.
- 1/2 cup water
- Chopped thyme springs (or 3 thyme leaves) 1 cup canned chicken stock
- Another 2 tblsp. of extra virgin olive oil
- 1/2 cup grated gouda cheese; 8 ounces sliced mushrooms
- Season with salt and black pepper to taste.

### Directions:

1. Heat the butter in a skillet large enough to accommodate your air fryer over medium heat, then add the onions and garlic, stirring constantly, and cook for 4 minutes.
2. Stir in the oats, water, salt, pepper, stock, and thyme before placing the mixture in the air fryer and cooking for 16 minutes at 360 degrees F.
3. To prepare the oatmeal and cheese, heat a pan with the olive oil over medium heat until hot. Add the mushrooms and cook for 3 minutes before adding them to the porridge and cheese. Divide the oats into bowls and serve for breakfast.
4. Enjoy!

The following are the nutritional values: calories 284, fat 8, fiber 8, carbohydrates 20, protein 17.

# RICE , ALMONDS AND RAISINS PUDDING

**Preparation time:** 5 minutes **Cooking time:** 8 minutes **Servings:** 4

## Ingredients:

- 1 cup brown rice, uncooked
- 1/2 cup shredded coconut1 quart of milk
- 2 quarts of water.
- 1/2 cup maple syrup, pure
- 1 pound raisins
- 1/4 cup sliced almonds
- Cinnamon powder, a pinch of it.

## Directions:

1. Place the rice in a large enough pan to fit your air fryer, add the water, and cook over medium-high heat until the rice is mushy.Drain the rice.
2. In a large mixing bowl, combine the milk, coconut chips, almonds, raisins, cinnamon, and maple syrup; stir well.Cook for 8 minutes at 360 degrees F in an air fryer.
3. Divide the rice pudding among the serving bowls and serve. Enjoy!

Calories: 251, fat: 6 g, fiber: 8 g, carbohydrates: 39 g, protein: 12 g

# DATES AND MILLET PUDDING

**Preparation time:** 10 minutes **Cooking time:** 15 minutes **Servings:** 4

## *Ingredients:*

- 14 ounces of whole milk
- 7 ounces of pure water.
- 2/3 cup of millet 4 pitted datesHoney used as a condiment

## Directions:

1. Place the millet in a pan that will fit your air fryer. Add the dates, milk, and water. Stir, and then place the pan in your air fryer and cook at 360 degrees F for 15 minutes.
2.
2. Divide the mixture between the plates and drizzle with honey before serving for breakfast.Enjoy!

The following are the nutritional values: calories 231, fat 6, fiber 6, carbohydrates 18, protein 6.

# AIR FRYER LUNCH RECIPES

# LUNCH EGG ROLLS

**Preparation time:** 10 minutes **Cooking time:** 15 minutes **Servings:** 4

## Ingredients:

- 1/2 cup mushrooms, chopped1/2 cup grated carrots2 tbsp. grated zucchini green onions, chopped 2 tbsp of soy sauce8 egg roll wrappers (for 8 egg rolls) 1/2 cups of mushrooms, chopped 12 cups of carrots, grated
- 1 lightly whisked egg
- 1 tbsp cornstarch (optional).

## Directions:

1. In a large mixing basin, combine the carrots, mushrooms, zucchini, green onions, and soy sauce, stirring well.
2. Lay out the egg roll wrappers on a work surface, divide the veggie mixture among them, and roll them tightly.
3. In a separate dish, whisk together the cornstarch and the egg until well combined. Brush the egg rolls with this mixture.
4. Seal the edges of the rolls and place them in a preheated air fryer for 15 minutes at 370 degrees F.
5. Prepare them on a platter and offer them as a side dish with your lunch. Enjoy!

Nutritional information 172 calories, 6 grams of fat, 6 grams of fiber, 8 grams of carbohydrates, and 7 grams of protein.

# VEGGIE TOAST

**Preparation time:** 10 minutes **Cooking time:** 15 minutes **Servings:** 4

## Ingredients:

- 1 red bell pepper, peeled and thinly sliced1 cup sliced cremini mushrooms 1 cup sliced cremini mushrooms
- 1 chopped yellow squash 2 thinly sliced green onions 1 chopped yellow squash
- 1 tbsp olive oil (extra virgin)4 slices of sourdough bread
- 2 tablespoons of melted butter (softened)
- 1/2 cup goat cheese, crumbled

## Directions:

1. Toss together the red bell pepper, mushrooms, squash, green onions, and oil in a large mixing bowl.Transfer the vegetables to an air fryer and cook at 350 degrees F for 10 minutes, shaking the fryer once, until the vegetables are tender.
2. Cook the bread slices at 350 degrees F for 5 minutes after spreading butter on them in an air fryer.
3. To serve, divide the veggie mixture among the bread slices and top with cheese crumbles.
4. Enjoy!

Nutritional information: 152 calories, 3 grams of fat, 4 grams of fiber, 7 grams of carbohydrates, and 2 grams of protein.

# STUFFED MUSHROOMS

**Preparation time:** 10 minutes **Cooking time:** 20 minutes **Servings:** 4

## Ingredients:

- 4 large Portobello mushroom tops (optional). 14 cups of ricotta cheese 1 tbsp olive oil (extra virgin)
- 5 tbsp parmesan cheese, grated 1 cup spinach, shredded
- A third of a cup of bread crumbs
- 14 teaspoon finely chopped rosemary

## Directions:

1. Toss the mushroom caps with the oil, then put them into your air fryer's basket and cook them for 2 minutes at 350 degrees F.
2. In the meantime, in a large mixing bowl, combine half of the parmesan with the ricotta, spinach, rosemary, and bread crumbs, stirring thoroughly.
3. Place the mushrooms in the air fryer basket once again and cook at 350 degrees Fahrenheit for 10 minutes. 3. Stuff the mushrooms with the mixture and sprinkle the remaining parmesan on top.
4. To serve them for lunch, divide them among plates and accompany them with a side salad. Enjoy!

Nutritional information: 152 calories, 4 grams of fat, 7 grams of fiber, 9 grams of carbohydrates, and 5 grams of protein.

**Preparation time:** 10 minutes **Cooking time:** 7 minutes **Servings:** 4

## Ingredients:

- pitas (four pitas)
- 1 tbsp olive oil (extra virgin)
- one-quarter cup pizza sauce
- 2 cups chopped canned mushrooms, 4 ounces sliced canned mushrooms
- 1/2 teaspoons of basil (dried), 2 green onions (chopped), 2 cups of mozzarella (grated), 12 teaspoons of basil
- 1 cup (optional) sliced grape tomatoes

## Directions:

1. Using your fingers, spread pizza sauce over each pita bread, then top with green onions and basil, then divide the mushrooms and cheese.
2. Arrange the pita pizzas in your air fryer and cook them for 7 minutes at 400°F.
3. Before serving, place tomato slices on top of each pizza and divide them among plates.Enjoy!

Nutritional information: 200 calories, 4 grams of fat, 6 grams of fiber, 7 grams of carbohydrates, and 3 grams of protein.

# LUNCH GNOCCHI

**Preparation time:** 10 minutes **Cooking time:** 17 minutes **Servings:** 4

## Ingredients:

- 1 finely sliced yellow onion1 tbsp olive oil (extra virgin)
- Gnocchi (about 16 oz.) 3-4 garlic cloves, minced
- 1/4 cup grated parmesan; 8 ounces spinach pesto

## Directions:

1. Prepare the gnocchi, onion, and garlic in a large mixing bowl, then transfer the mixture to an air fryer pan and cook at 400 degrees F for 10 minutes. 2.
2. Stir in the pesto and continue to cook for 7 minutes at 350°F.
3. Divide the mixture among the serving dishes and serve for lunch.Enjoy!

Nutritional information: 200 calories, 4 grams of fat, 4 grams of fiber, 12 grams of carbohydrates, and 4 grams of protein.

# SCALLOPS AND DILL

**Preparation time:** 10 minutes **Cooking time:** 5 minutes **Servings:** 4

## *Ingredients:*

- Two cups of debearded sea scallops 1 teaspoon lemon juiceone pound sea scallops
- 2 teaspoons extra-virgin olive oil, 1 teaspoon finely chopped dill
- Season with salt and black pepper to taste.

## Directions:

1. In your air fryer, combine the scallops with the dill, oil, salt, pepper, and lemon juice, cover, and cook at 360 degrees F for 5 minutes until done.
2. Discard those that have not been opened, and divide the scallops and dill sauce among the dishes for lunch.
3. Enjoy!

Nutritional information: 152 calories, 4 grams of fat, 7 grams of fiber, 19 grams of carbohydrates, and 4 grams of protein.

# HOT BACON SANDWICHES

**Preparation time:** 10 minutes **Cooking time:** 7 minutes **Servings:** 4

## *Ingredients:*

- A third cup of barbecue sauce
- Honey (about 2 tablespoons)
- Bacon (boiled and chopped into thirds): 8 slices bacon1 peeled and sliced red bell pepper
- One small yellow bell pepper, thinly sliced, divided into three pita pockets, each half
- 15-cup butter lettuce leaves, divided into quarters; 2 tomatoes, thinly sliced

## Directions:

1. In a large mixing bowl, whisk together the barbecue sauce and honey until thoroughly combined.
2. Brush the bacon and all of the bell peppers with some of this mixture, then place them in your air fryer and cook for 4 minutes at 350 degrees Fahrenheit.
3. Shake the fryer and cook them for a further 2 minutes.
4. Stuff pita pockets with the bacon mixture, as well as tomatoes and lettuce, and then put the remaining barbecue sauce on top and serve for lunch.
5. Enjoy!

186 calories, 6 grams of fat, 9 grams of fiber, 14 grams of carbohydrates, and 4 grams of protein.

# FISH AND CHIPS

**Preparation time:** 10 minutes **Cooking time:** 12 minutes **Servings:** 2

## Ingredients:

- 2 medium cod fillets, skinless and boneless, cooked in a skillet with salt and black pepper to taste.
- 1/4 cup buttermilk
- 3 cups drained and cooled kettle chips

## Directions:

1. Combine the fish, salt, pepper, and buttermilk in a large mixing bowl; toss well and set aside for 5 minutes.
2. Place the chips in a food processor and pulse until they are crushed. Spread the chips on a platter.
3. Place the fish on top and press down firmly on all sides.
4. Place the fish in the basket of your air fryer and cook at 400°F for 12 minutes.
5. Prepare a hot meal for your guests.Enjoy!

The following are the nutritional values: calories 271, fat 7, fiber 9, carbohydrates 14, protein 4.

# HASH BROWN TOASTS

**Preparation time:** 10 minutes **Cooking time:** 7 minutes **Servings:** 4

## *Ingredients:*

- 4 hash brown patties, defrosted from the freezer. 1 tbsp olive oil (extra virgin)
- 1/4 cup chopped cherry tomatoes
- grated 2 tbsp. shredded parmesan cheese3 tablespoons shredded mozzarella
- 1 tbsp. balsamic vinegar, 1 tbsp. minced basil, 1 tbsp. olive oil

## Directions:

1. Place the hash brown patties in the air fryer, drizzle with oil, and cook for 7 minutes at 400 degrees F, or until crispy.
2. In a large mixing bowl, combine the tomatoes, mozzarella, parmesan, vinegar, and basil. Stir thoroughly.
3. Assemble the hash brown patties on plates and top each with a tomato mixture before serving them for lunch.
4. Enjoy!

199 calories, 3 grams of fat, 8 grams of fiber, 12 grams of carbohydrates, and 4 grams of protein.

# DELICIOUS BEEF CUBES

**Preparation time:** 10 minutes **Cooking time:** 12 minutes **Servings:** 4

## Ingredients:

- 1 pound sirloin steak, cubed
- Jarred spaghetti sauce (about 16 ounces) Bread crumbs (about 1/2 cup) 2 tbsp olive oil (extra-virgin)
- 1/2 teaspoons of ground marjoram, preferably dried.
- ready-to-serve white rice that has already been cooked.

## Directions:

1. In a large mixing bowl, combine the meat cubes with the pasta sauce and toss thoroughly.
2. In a separate bowl, combine the bread crumbs, marjoram, and oil, stirring thoroughly.
3. Coat the beef cubes with this mixture and place them in your air fryer at 360 degrees F for 12 minutes.
4. Arrange the mixture on individual plates and serve with white rice on the side. Enjoy!

The following are the nutritional values: calories 271, fat 6, fiber 9, carbohydrates 18, protein 12.

# PASTA SALAD

**Preparation time:** 10 minutes **Cooking time:** 12 minutes **Servings:** 6

## Ingredients:

- 1 halved and roughly diced zucchini1 medium orange bell pepper, finely chopped
- These are thinly sliced.1 small green bell pepper1 small red bell pepper1/2 cup coarsely chopped red onion
- To taste, season with salt and freshly ground black pepper.4 ounces of brown mushrooms, halved
- 1/4 tsp. Italian seasoning (optional)
- 1 pound of pre-cooked penne rigate1 cup cherry tomatoes, peeled and halved
- 1/2 cup pitted and halved kalamata olives
- 1 tablespoon extra virgin olive oil
- Balsamic vinegar (three tablespoons) 2 tbsp. fresh basil (chopped)

### Directions:

1. In a large mixing bowl, combine the zucchini, mushrooms, orange bell pepper, green bell pepper, red onion, salt, pepper, Italian seasoning, and oil; toss well. Transfer the zucchini to an air fryer preheated to 380 degrees F and cook for 12 minutes, or until the zucchini is tender.
2. Cooked vegetables, cherry tomatoes, olives, vinegar, and basil should all be combined in a big salad bowl before serving for lunch.
3. Enjoy!

Nutritional information: 200 calories, 5 grams of fat, 8 grams of fiber, 10 grams of carbohydrates, and 6 grams of protein.

# TASTY CHEESEBURGERS

**Preparation time:** 10 minutes **Cooking time:** 20 minutes **Servings:** 2

## Ingredients:

- 12 oz. lean beef, preferably ground, 4 tbsp. ketchup (optional)
- 3 tablespoons finely diced yellow onion2 teaspoons of Dijon mustard.
- Season with salt and black pepper to taste. 4 pieces of cheddar cheese, sliced
- 2 burger buns, cut in half.

## Directions:

1. In a large mixing bowl, combine the meat, onion, ketchup, mustard, salt, and pepper. Stir well and form 4 patties from the mixture.
2. Divide the cheese evenly between the two patties and top with the remaining two burgers.
3. Fry them for 20 minutes in an air fryer preheated to 370 degrees F.
4. Place the cheeseburger on the bottom of two bun halves, then top with the remaining two, and serve for lunch.
5. Enjoy!

Nutritional values: calories 261, fat 6 g, fiber 10 g, carbohydrates 20 g, protein 6 g.

# TURKISH KOFTAS

**Preparation time:** 10 minutes **Cooking time:** 15 minutes **Servings:** 2

## Ingredients:

- 1 finely chopped leek
- 2 tbsp (optional) crumbled feta cheese
- 2 tablespoons ground cumin 1 tablespoon chopped mint 1/2 pound lean beef minced 1 tablespoon cumin
- 1 tablespoon chopped parsley1 garlic clove, minced1 teaspoon olive oil
- Season with salt and black pepper to taste.

## Directions:

1. In a large mixing bowl, combine the meat, the leek, the cheese, and the seasonings (cumin, mint, parsley, garlic, salt, and pepper). Form your koftas and arrange them on sticks.
2. Place the koftas in an air fryer that has been preheated to 360 degrees F and cook for about 15 minutes.
3. For lunch, serve them with a side salad on a bed of lettuce. Enjoy!

The following are the nutritional values: calories 281, fat 7, fiber 8, carbohydrates 17, protein 6.

# CHINESE PORK LUNCH MIX

**Preparation time:** 10 minutes **Cooking time:** 12 minutes **Servings:** 4

## Ingredients:

- Two quail eggs
- Pork, sliced into medium-sized pieces, 2 pounds Optional: 1 cup cornstarch
- Optional: 1 teaspoon sesame oil
- Season with salt and black pepper to taste and add a sprinkle of five-spice powder from China.
- 3 tblsp. extra-virgin olive oil.
- For the sauce, use a sweet tomato sauce.

## Directions:

1. In a large mixing bowl, combine the five spices with the salt, pepper, and cornstarch, stirring constantly.
2. In a separate dish, whisk together the eggs and sesame oil until thoroughly combined.
3. Dredge the pork cubes in the cornstarch mixture, then dip them in the egg mixture, and then set them in the air fryer that has been greased with canola oil.
4. Cook for 12 minutes at 340°F, shaking the fryer once during the cooking time.
5. For lunch, serve the pork chops with the sweet tomato sauce on the side. Enjoy!

Nutritional information 320 calories, 8 grams of fat, 12 grams of fiber, 20 grams of carbohydrates, and 5 grams of protein.

# BEEF LUNCH MEATBALLS

**Preparation time:** 10 minutes **Cooking time:** 15 minutes **Servings:** 4

## Ingredients:

- 1/2 pound of beef that has been ground
- 1/2 pound of Italian sausage, finely minced.
- 1/2 teaspoon of garlic powder (optional).
- 1/2 teaspoons of onion powder (optional)
- Season with salt and black pepper to taste.
- 1/2 cups of cheddar cheese, grated mashed potatoes to be used as a side dish.

## Directions:

1. In a large mixing bowl, combine the beef, sausage, garlic powder, onion powder, salt, pepper, and cheese. Thoroughly combine the ingredients. Form 16 meatballs from the mixture.
2. Place the meatballs in your air fryer and cook them for 15 minutes at 370 degrees Fahrenheit.
3. Serve your meatballs with mashed potatoes on the side to complete the meal. Enjoy!

Nutritional information: 333 calories, 23 grams of fat, 1 gram of fiber, 8 grams of carbohydrates, and 20 grams of protein.

# EASY HOT DOGS

**Preparation time:** 10 minutes **Cooking time:** 7 minutes **Servings:** 2

## Ingredients:

- 2 (optional) hot dog buns2 frankfurters
- 1 tbsp (optional) Dijon mustard
- 2 tbsp (optional) grated cheddar cheese

## Directions:

1. Cook hot dogs for 5 minutes in an air fryer that has been preheated to 390 degrees F.
2. Divide hot dogs among buns, top with mustard and cheese, and return to the air fryer for another 2 minutes at 390 degrees F.
3. Place it on the lunch table.Enjoy!

211 calories, 3 grams of fat, 8 grams of fiber, 12 grams of carbohydrates, and 4 grams of protein.

# PROSCIUTTO SANDWICH

**Preparation time:** 10 minutes **Cooking time:** 5 minutes **Servings:** 1

## Ingredients:

- Sourdough bread, 2 slices
- 2 pieces of mozzarella cheese.
- 2 tomato slices
- Two slices of prosciutto
- 2 basil leaves (optional)
- 1 tsp olive oil (extra-virgin)
- a pinch of salt and freshly ground black pepper

## Directions:

1. Arrange the mozzarella and prosciutto on a slice of ciabatta bread.
2. Season with salt and pepper, then cook for 5 minutes at 400 degrees F in your air fryer.
3. Spoon oil over the prosciutto, add the tomato and basil, cover with the second bread slice, and split the sandwich in half before serving. Enjoy!

Nutritional information: 172 calories, 3 grams of fat, 7 grams of fiber, 9 grams of carbohydrates, and 5 grams of protein.

# LENTILS FRITTERS

**Preparation time:** 10 minutes **Cooking time:** 10 minutes **Servings:** 2

## *Ingredients:*

- 1 cup of yellow lentils, soaked for 1 hour in water, then drained, 1 cup
- 1 peeled and diced hot chili pepper
- Ginger, 1 inch piece, finely grated
- 1/2 teaspoon turmeric powder1 tablespoon garam masala (chili powder)
- 1 tsp (optional) baking powder
- Season with salt and black pepper to taste. 2 tsp olive oil (extra-virgin)
- one-third cup of water
- 1/2 cup cilantro, chopped
- 1 and 1/2 cups of spinach, chopped. 4 minced garlic cloves
- 3/4 cup chopped red onion, mint chutney (served separately)

## Directions:

1. In a blender, combine the lentils, chili pepper, ginger, turmeric, garam masala, baking powder, salt, pepper, olive oil, water, cilantro, spinach, onion, and garlic until well combined. Form medium-sized balls out of the mixture using a cookie scoop.
2. Place everything in a preheated air fryer at 400 degrees F for 10 minutes, or until the chicken is cooked through.
3. 0 For lunch, serve your vegetable fritters with a side of salad. Enjoy!

Nutritional information 142 calories, 2 grams of fat, 8 grams of fiber, 12 grams of carbohydrates, and 4 grams of protein.

# LUNCH POTATO SALAD

**Preparation time:** 10 minutes **Cooking time:** 25 minutes **Servings:** 4

## *Ingredients:*

- split, as well as 2 tablespoons extra-virgin olive oil
- season with salt and black pepper to taste 2 green onions, peeled and cut
- 3 tbsp fresh lemon juice1 finely sliced red bell pepper
- Mustard (three tablespoons)

## Directions:

1. Toss the potatoes in the air fryer basket with half of the olive oil, salt, and pepper.Cook for 25 minutes at 350°F, shaking the fryer halfway through.
2. Toss the onions, bell pepper, and roasted potatoes together in a large mixing bowl.
3. Place lemon juice in a small mixing basin with the remaining oil and mustard. Whisk vigorously.
4. Toss this into the potato salad and serve as a lunch side dish.Enjoy!

211 calories, 6 grams of fat, 8 grams of fiber, 12 grams of carbohydrates, and 4 grams of protein.

# STEAKS AND CABBAGE

**Preparation time:** 10 minutes **Cooking time:** 10 minutes **Servings:** 4

## Ingredients:

- 1/2 pound sirloin steak, thinly sliced (in strips). 2 tablespoons cornstarch (optional)
- 1 tablespoon of ground peanut oil.
- 1 chopped yellow bell pepper 2 chopped green onions 2 cups chopped green cabbage 1 chopped yellow bell pepper
- 2 garlic cloves, peeled and minced.
- Season with salt and black pepper to taste.

## Directions:

1. In a large mixing bowl, combine the cabbage, salt, pepper, and peanut oil; toss well. 2. Then transfer to an air fryer basket and cook at 370 degrees F for 4 minutes, then transfer to a large mixing bowl.
2. In the air fryer, combine the steak strips, green onions, bell pepper, garlic, salt, and pepper, and cook for 5 minutes, or until the steak is cooked through.
3. Pour over the cabbage and mix to combine. Divide it across plates and serve it for lunch. Enjoy!

The following are the nutritional values: calories 282, fat 6, fiber 8, carbohydrates 14, protein 6.

# TURKEY CAKES

**Preparation time:** 10 minutes **Cooking time:** 10 minutes **Servings:** 4

## Ingredients:

- Six sliced mushrooms (chopped)
- Optional: 1 teaspoon garlic powderOptional: 1 teaspoon onion powder
- Season with salt and black pepper to taste.
- 1 and 1/4 pounds turkey meat, ground Cooking spray 1 and 14 pounds turkey meat, ground
- Tomato sauce to be used as a condiment

## Directions:

1. Formalized paraphraseIn a blender, puree together the mushrooms, salt, and pepper until completely combined. Transfer to a bowl.
2. Combine the turkey, onion powder, garlic powder, salt, and pepper in a large mixing bowl and shape the mixture into cakes.
3. Spray them with cooking spray, place them in your air fryer, and cook at 320°F for 10 minutes, or until crispy.
4. Garnish with tomato sauce on the side, and serve with a nice side salad on the side.
5. Enjoy!

Nutritional information 202 calories, 6 grams of fat, 3 grams of fiber, 17 grams of carbohydrates, and 10 grams of protein.

**Preparation time:** 10 minutes **Cooking time:** 8 minutes **Servings:** 6

## *Ingredients:*

- ravioli with cheese (around 20 ounces) 10 ounces marinara sauce (optional) 1 tablespoon extra-virgin olive oil
- 1 cup buttermilk (optional)
- 2 cups toasted bread crumbs
- 1/4 cup parmesan cheese, grated

## Directions:

1. Place the buttermilk in one basin and the breadcrumbs in another one.
2. Dip ravioli in buttermilk, then in breadcrumbs, and set them on a baking sheet in the air fryer to cook until golden brown.
3. Drizzle olive oil over them and bake at 400 degrees F for 5 minutes, then divide them onto plates and sprinkle parmesan on top before serving for lunch.
4. Enjoy!

Nutritional information: 270 calories, 12 grams of fat, 6 grams of fiber, 30 grams of carbohydrates, and 15 grams of protein

# BEEF STEW

**Preparation time:** 10 minutes **Cooking time:** 20 minutes **Servings:** 4

## Ingredients:

- chopped into medium-sized chunks 2 pounds of beef meat. 2 carrots, peeled and chopped.
- potatoes, chopped (four potatoes).
- Season with salt and black pepper to taste and add 1 quart of vegetable stock.
- 1/2 tsp smoked paprika, 1 tbsp finely chopped thyme

## Directions:

1. Toss the beef with the carrots, potatoes, and stock in a dish that will fit in your air fryer's basket before placing it in the air fryer's basket and cooking it for 20 minutes at 375 degrees Fahrenheit, or until the beef is no longer pink.
2. Divide the mixture into bowls and serve for lunch right away.
3. Enjoy!

260 calories, 5 grams of fat, 8 grams of fiber, 20 grams of carbohydrates, and 22 grams of protein.

# SPECIAL LUNCH SEAFOOD STEW

**Preparation time:** 10 minutes **Cooking time:** 20 minutes **Servings:** 4

## Ingredients:

- 5 ounces of white rice. 2 ounces (peas) brown rice (5 oz.)
- 14 ounces white wine, 1 finely chopped red bell pepper1 small red bell pepper
- 3 oz. of pure water
- squid chunks (about 2 ounces). Mussels (about 7 ounces)
- 2 pound fillet of sea bass (skinless, boneless, and diced)3 oz. sea bass fillet,
    - pounds of shrimp and 4 clams (3.5 ounces)
- 4 crayfish
- Season with salt and black pepper to taste. 1 tbsp olive oil (extra virgin)

## Directions:

1. Cook the sea bass with the other seafood in your air fryer's pan. Add the crayfish and the clams to the pan. 3. Cook for 5 minutes more on high heat.
2. Toss in the oil, salt, and pepper to coat the vegetables.
3. In a large mixing bowl, combine the peas, salt, pepper, bell pepper, and rice, stirring constantly.
4. Pour this mixture over the seafood, along with the wine and water, and place the pan in the air fryer for 20 minutes at 400 degrees F, stirring halfway through.
5. Divide into bowls and serve as a snack or meal for lunch.
6. Enjoy!

Nutritional information 300 calories, 12 grams of fat, 2 grams of fiber, 23 grams of carbohydrates, and 25 grams of protein.

# AIR FRIED THAI SALAD

**Preparation time:** 10 minutes **Cooking time:** 5 minutes **Servings:** 4

## Ingredients:

- 1 cup (optional) shredded carrots
- 1 cup red cabbage, finely shredded
- a pinch of salt and freshly ground black pepper handful of finely chopped cilantro
- 1 finely sliced small cucumber1 freshly squeezed lime
- 2 teaspoons of curry paste (red curry)
- 12 large shrimp that have been boiled, peeled, and deveined

## Directions:

1. In a pan that fits your air fryer, combine the cabbage, carrots, cucumber, and shrimp; stir well. Place the pan in your air fryer and cook for 5 minutes at 360 degrees F.
2. Toss in the salt, pepper, cilantro, lime juice, and red curry paste until well combined, then divide among plates and serve immediately.
3. Enjoy!

Nutritional information 172 calories, 5 grams of fat, 7 grams of fiber, 8 grams of carbohydrates, and 5 grams of protein.

# TURKEY BURGERS

**Preparation time:** 10 minutes **Cooking time:** 8 minutes **Servings:** 4

## *Ingredients:*

- ground turkey meat. 1 finely chopped shallot1 pound of ground turkey meat.
- A little sprinkling of extra-virgin olive oil
- lime juice, 2 teaspoons2 teaspoons cilantro 1 small jalapeo pepper, chopped
- 1 lime, grated and zest
- Season with salt and black pepper to taste. 1 tsp cumin seeds (finely ground)
- 1 teaspoon of paprika (sweet) guacamole to be used for serving.

## Directions:

1. In a large mixing bowl, combine the turkey meat with the salt, pepper, cumin, paprika, shallot, jalapeo, lime juice, and zest. Stir well. Form burgers from the turkey meat mixture, drizzle the oil over them, and cook them at 370 degrees F for 8 minutes on each side.
2. Divide the mixture among the dishes and serve with guacamole on the side.
3. Enjoy!

200 calories, 12 grams of fat, 0 grams of fiber, 0 grams of carbohydrates, and 12 grams of protein.

# SALMON AND ASPARAGUS

**Preparation time:** 10 minutes **Cooking time:** 23 minutes **Servings:** 4

## Ingredients:

- 1 pound asparagus, trimmed1 tbsp olive oil (extra virgin)
- with a sprinkle of smoked paprika (sweet).
- Season with salt and black pepper to taste and add a pinch of garlic powder (optional).
- A pinch of cayenne pepper (optional)
- 3 tbsp of smoked salmon4 oz. red bell pepper, cut into halves

## Directions:

1. Cook at 390° F for 8 minutes, then flip and cook for another 8 minutes on a lined baking sheet that fits your air fryer. 1. Arrange asparagus spears and bell pepper on a baking sheet lined with parchment paper that fits your air fryer.2. Add salt, pepper, garlic powder, paprika, olive oil, and cayenne pepper to taste.Place it in the air fryer.
2. Add the salmon and cook for 5 minutes more before dividing between plates and serving.
3. Enjoy!

90 calories, 1 gram of fat, 1 gram of fiber, 1 gram of carbohydrate, and 4 grams of protein.

# CHICKEN AND CORN CASSEROLE

**Preparation time:** 10 minutes **Cooking time:** 30 minutes **Servings:** 6

## *Ingredients:*

- 1 cup of boiled chicken broth, 2 tablespoons of garlic powder (optional),
- Season with salt and black pepper to taste. 6 oz. coconut milk in a can
- Green lentils (about 1 and 1/2 cups)
- Chicken breasts, skinless, boneless, and cubed (about 2 pounds) A third cup of cilantro, finely chopped
- 3 cups boiled corn
- 3 large handfuls of spinach.
- 3 green onions, thinly sliced.

### Directions:

1. In a pan large enough to fit your air fryer, combine the stock, coconut milk, salt, pepper, garlic powder, chicken, and lentils. 2. Cook until the chicken and lentils are done.
2. In a large mixing bowl, combine the corn, green onions, cilantro, and spinach, then transfer to an air fryer and cook at 350 degrees F for 30 minutes.
3. Enjoy!

Nutrition: 345 calories, 12 grams of fat, 10 grams of fiber, 20 grams of carbohydrates, and 44 grams of protein.

# AIR FRYER SIDE DISH RECIPES

# POTATO WEDGES

**Preparation time:** 10 minutes **Cooking time:** 25 minutes **Servings:** 4

## *Ingredients:*

- 2 potatoes, peeled and sliced into wedges. 1 tbsp olive oil (extra virgin)
- Season with salt and black pepper to taste. Sour cream (three tablespoons)
- 2 teaspoons sauce (sweet chili sauce)

## Directions:

1. In a large mixing bowl, combine the potato wedges with the oil, salt, and pepper, toss well, and transfer to the air fryer basket. Cook them at 360 degrees F for 25 minutes, flipping them once during the cooking process.
2. Arrange potato wedges on plates, drizzle with sour cream and chili sauce, and serve as a side dish to accompany the main course.
3. Enjoy!

Calories: 171, fat: 8 g, fiber: 9 g, carbohydrates: 18 g, protein: 7 g

# MUSHROOM SIDE DISH

**Preparation time:** 10 minutes **Cooking time:** 8 minutes **Servings:** 4

## *Ingredients:*

- 10 button mushrooms, stems removed, 1 tbsp Italian seasoning (optional).
- Season with salt and black pepper to taste.
- 2 tbsp. shredded cheddar cheese1 tbsp olive oil (extra virgin)
- 2 tbsp. grated mozzarella1 tablespoon finely chopped dill

## Directions:

1. In a large mixing bowl, combine the mushrooms, Italian seasoning, salt, pepper, oil, and dill, and toss well.
2. Arrange the mushrooms in the air fryer's basket, sprinkle mozzarella and cheddar cheese on top of each, and cook for 8 minutes at 360 degrees Fahrenheit.
3. Arrange them on plates as a side dish, and serve them immediately. Enjoy!

The following are the nutritional values: calories 241, fat 7, fiber 8, carbohydrates 14, protein 6.

# HASSELBACK POTATOES

**Preparation time:** 10 minutes **Cooking time:** 20 minutes **Servings:** 2

## Ingredients:

- 2 potatoes, peeled and thinly sliced almost all the way across the length of the potato.
- 2 tbsp olive oil (extra-virgin)
- 1 teaspoon garlic, finely minced
- Season with salt and black pepper to taste.
- 1/2 teaspoons of dried oregano leaves
- 1/2 teaspoon of fresh basil (or dried basil)
- 1/2 teaspoon of paprika (sweet)

### Directions:

1. In a large mixing bowl, whisk together the oil, garlic, salt, pepper, oregano, basil, and paprika until thoroughly combined.
2. Rub the potatoes with the mixture, then place them in the air fryer basket and cook for 20 minutes at 360 degrees F.3.
3. Arrange them on plates and serve them as a side dish with the main course. Enjoy!

Nutritional information: 172 calories, 6 grams of fat, 6 grams of fiber, 9 grams of carbohydrates, and 6 grams of protein.

# BRUSSELS SPROUTS SIDE DISH

**Preparation time:** 10 minutes **Cooking time:** 15 minutes **Servings:** 4

## Ingredients:

- 1 pound Brussels sprouts, trimmed and halved (optional)Season with salt and black pepper to taste.
- 6 tsp olive oil, extra-virgin
- 1/2 teaspoon finely chopped fresh thyme
- Optional: 1/2 cup mayonnaise
- Crushed roasted garlic (about 2 teaspoons)

## Directions:

1. In your air fryer, combine the Brussels sprouts with the salt, pepper, and oil, toss well, and cook for 15 minutes at 390 degrees F.
2. In the meantime, whisk together the thyme, mayonnaise, and garlic in a large mixing bowl.
3. Arrange the Brussels sprouts in individual dishes and sprinkle with garlic sauce before serving as a side dish.
4. Enjoy!

Nutritional information: 172 calories, 6 grams of fat, 8 grams of fiber, 12 grams of carbohydrates, and 6 grams of protein

# ROASTED PUMPKIN

**Preparation time:** 10 minutes **Cooking time:** 12 minutes **Servings:** 4

## Ingredients:

- pumpkin (between 1 and 1/2 pounds), deseeded, diced, and coarsely chopped.
- 3 garlic cloves, peeled and minced.
- 1 tbsp olive oil (extra virgin)A pinch of sea salt is a good idea.
- A pinch of brown sugar is used in this recipe.
- 1 tsp freshly ground nutmegCinnamon powder, a pinch of it.

### Directions:

1. In the basket of your air fryer, combine the pumpkin, garlic, oil, salt, brown sugar, cinnamon, and nutmeg, toss well, and cook at 370 degrees F for 12 minutes, or until the pumpkin is tender.
2. Divide the mixture across plates and serve as a side dish. Enjoy!

Nutritional information: 200 calories, 5 grams of fat, 4 grams of fiber, 7 grams of carbohydrates, and 4 grams of protein.

# PARMESAN MUSHROOMS

**Preparation time:** 10 minutes **Cooking time:** 15 minutes **Servings:** 3

## Ingredients:

- 9 button mushroom tops (about)
- 1 beaten egg white3 crumbled cream cracker slices
- 1 tsp Italian seasoning2 tbsp. finely grated parmesan cheese
- a pinch of salt and freshly ground black pepper1 tablespoon of melted butter (or margarine)

## Directions:

1. In a large mixing bowl, combine crackers, egg white, parmesan, Italian seasoning, butter, salt, and pepper; thoroughly combine. Stuff mushrooms with the cracker mixture.
2. Place the mushrooms in the basket of your air fryer and cook for 15 minutes at 360°F, or until soft.
3. Divide the mixture among plates and serve with your meal as a side dish.Enjoy!

124 calories, 4 grams of fat, 4 grams of fiber, 7 grams of carbohydrates, and 3 grams of protein.

# EGGPLANT SIDE DISH

**Preparation time:** 10 minutes **Cooking time:** 10 minutes **Servings:** 4

## Ingredients:

- 8 baby eggplants, scooped out of the middle and the pulp set aside
- Season with salt and black pepper to taste.
- A pinch of oregano leaves, preferably dried
- 1 diced green bell pepper 1 tbsp tomato paste 1 tbsp olive oil
- 1 bunch finely chopped coriander leaves
- 1/2 teaspoons of garlic powder (optional) 1 tbsp olive oil (extra virgin)
- 1 finely sliced small yellow onion1 peeled and chopped tomato

## Directions:

1. Heat the oil in a pan over medium heat, then add the onion and cook, stirring constantly, for 1 minute.
2. Stir in the remaining ingredients (salt and pepper), then continue to cook for another 1-2 minutes before removing from the heat and allowing to cool completely.3.
3. Stuff the eggplants with the mixture, place in the air fryer basket, and cook for 8 minutes at 360°F.
4. Arrange the eggplants on plates as a side dish and serve immediately. Enjoy!

Nutritional information: 200 calories, 3 grams of fat, 7 grams of fiber, 12 grams of carbohydrates, and 4 grams of protein.

# MUSHROOMS AND SOUR CREAM

**Preparation time:** 10 minutes **Cooking time:** 10 minutes **Servings:** 6

## Ingredients:

- Chop up 2 bacon pieces and 1 yellow onion for this recipe.
- 1 chopped green bell pepper 24 mushrooms, stems removed1 red bell pepper, chopped. 1 carrot, peeled and grated.
- 1/2 cup sour cream (optional)
- 1 cup grated cheddar cheeseSalt and black pepper to taste 1 cup grated mozzarella cheese

## Directions:

1. Heat a large skillet over medium-high heat, then add the bacon, onion, bell pepper, and carrot, stirring constantly and cooking for 1 minute.
2. Cook for 1 minute longer, stirring constantly, before removing from heat and allowing to cool completely.
3. Stuff the mushrooms with the mixture, then top with cheese and bake for 8 minutes at 360°F.
4. Divide the mixture among plates and serve as a side dish with your meal. Enjoy!

Nutritional information 211 calories, 4 grams of fat, 7 grams of fiber, 8 grams of carbohydrates, and 3 grams of protein.

# CREAMY BRUSSELS SPROUTS

**Preparation time:** 10 minutes **Cooking time:** 25 minutes **Servings:** 8

## Ingredients:

- Half-halved Brussels sprouts (around 3 pounds) A little sprinkling of extra-virgin olive oil
- 1 pound diced cooked bacon
- 4 tbsp. butter
- 3 shallots, peeled and sliced.
- 1 quart of milk
- 2 quarts of thick cream.
- 1/4 teaspoon ground nutmeg
- 3 tablespoons of horseradish that has been prepared

## Directions:

1. preheat your air fryer to 370°F.Toss the Brussels sprouts in the oil and season with salt and pepper when it has been preheated.
2. Add the butter, shallots, heavy cream, milk, nutmeg, and horseradish and continue to cook for another 25 minutes, or until the vegetables are tender.
3. Divide the mixture among plates and serve with your meal as a side dish.Enjoy!

Nutritional information 214 calories, 5 grams of fat, 8 grams of fiber, 12 grams of carbohydrates, and 5 grams of protein.

# HERBED TOMATOES

**Preparation time:** 10 minutes **Cooking time:** 15 minutes **Servings:** 4

## Ingredients:

- 4 large tomatoes, halved, with the insides scooped out
- season with salt and black pepper to your liking
- 1 tbsp olive oil (extra virgin)2 garlic cloves, peeled and minced.
- 1/2 teaspoon finely chopped fresh thyme

## Directions:

1. Prepare the tomatoes in your air fryer by tossing them with salt and pepper, olive oil, garlic, and thyme, then cooking them for 15 minutes at 390 degrees F.
2. Divide the mixture between plates and serve as a side dish.Enjoy!

The following are the nutritional values: calories 112, fat 1, fiber 3, carbohydrates 4, protein 4.

# ROASTED PEPPERS

**Preparation time:** 10 minutes **Cooking time:** 20 minutes **Servings:** 4

## Ingredients:

- 1 tbsp roja paprika (sweet)1 tbsp olive oil (extra virgin)
- 4 medium-sized red bell peppers, sliced into medium-sized strips.
- 4 green bell peppers, thinly sliced into medium-length strips.
- 4 yellow bell peppers, thinly sliced into medium-length strips.
- 1 finely sliced small yellow onion
- Season with salt and black pepper to taste.

## Directions:

1. In a large mixing bowl, combine red bell peppers with green and yellow bell peppers.
2. In a large mixing bowl, combine the paprika, oil, onion, salt, and pepper and bake for 20 minutes at 350 degrees F.
3. Divide the mixture among plates and serve with your meal as a side dish.Enjoy!

Nutritional information 142 calories, 4 grams of fat, 4 grams of fiber, 7 grams of carbohydrates, and 4 grams of protein.

# CREAMY ENDIVES

**Preparation time:** 10 minutes **Cooking time:** 10 minutes **Servings:** 6

## Ingredients:

- 6 endives, trimmed and cut in half (see recipe). Optional: 1 teaspoon garlic powder
- 1/2 cup plain Greek yogurt
- 1 teaspoon curry powder
- Season with salt and black pepper to taste. 3 tbsp lemon juice (freshly squeezed)

**Directions:**

1. Mix together endives, garlic powder, yogurt, curry powder, salt, pepper, and lemon juice in a large mixing basin until well combined.
2. Set aside for 10 minutes before transferring to your preheated air fryer, which should be set to 350°F.
3. Prepare endives according to package directions for 10 minutes, then split them among plates and serve as a side dish.
4. Enjoy!

Nutritional information 100 calories, 2 grams of fat, 2 grams of fiber, 7 grams of carbohydrates, and 4 grams of protein.

# DELICIOUS ROASTED CARROTS

**Preparation time:** 10 minutes **Cooking time:** 20 minutes **Servings:** 4

## Ingredients:

- Baby carrots (around a pound)
- 2 tsp olive oil (extra-virgin)
- Herb of Provence (one teaspoon)
- 4 tbsp. freshly squeezed orange juice

## Directions:

1. In the basket of your air fryer, combine the carrots, herbs de Provence, oil, and orange juice; stir to combine, and cook at 320 degrees F for about 20 minutes.
2. Divide the mixture across plates and serve as a side dish. Enjoy!

Nutritional values: 112 calories, 2 fat grams, 3 carbohydrates, and 3 protein grams.

# VERMOUTH MUSHROOMS

**Preparation time:** 10 minutes **Cooking time:** 25 minutes **Servings:** 4

## Ingredients:

- 1 tbsp olive oil (extra virgin)
- 2 pounds of white button mushrooms.
- The white vermouth (about 2 tablespoons)
- 2 tablespoons of herbs de Provence (or equivalent) 2 garlic cloves, peeled and minced.

## Directions:

1. In your air fryer, combine the oil with the mushrooms, herbs de Provence, and garlic, toss, and cook for 20 minutes at 350 degrees F.
2. Stir in the vermouth and cook for another 5 minutes.
3. Divide the mixture among plates and serve with your meal as a side dish.Enjoy!

Nutritional information: 121 calories, 2 grams of fat, 5 grams of fiber, 7 grams of carbohydrates, and 4 grams of protein.

# ROASTED PARSNIPS

**Preparation time:** 10 minutes **Cooking time:** 40 minutes **Servings:** 6

## Ingredients:

- 2 pounds peeled and chopped parsnips into medium-sized bits into 2 pounds peeled and chopped parsnips
- 2 tablespoons of maple syrup (optional)
- 1-tablespoon of fresh or dried parsley flakes 1 tbsp olive oil (extra virgin)

## Directions:

1. Preheat your air fryer to 360°F and add the oil, heating it as well.
2. Add the parsnips, parsley flakes, and maple syrup and cook for 40 minutes, or until tender.
3. Divide the mixture among plates and serve with your meal as a side dish.Enjoy!

124 calories, 3 grams of fat, 3 grams of fiber, 7 grams of carbohydrates, and 4 grams of protein.

# GLAZED BEETS

**Preparation time:** 10 minutes **Cooking time:** 40 minutes **Servings:** 8

## Ingredients:

- 3 pounds of tiny beets, peeled and chopped.
- 4 tablespoons of maple syrup (optional)
- 1 tbsp (optional) duck fat

## Directions:

1. Preheat the air fryer to 360°F, then add the duck fat and heat it through.
2. Toss in the beets and maple syrup and cook for 40 minutes, stirring occasionally.
3. Divide the mixture among plates and serve with your meal as a side dish.Enjoy!

Nutritional information: 121 calories, 3 grams of fat, 2 grams of fiber, 3 grams of carbohydrates, and 4 grams of protein.

# ROASTED EGGPLANT

**Preparation time:** 10 minutes **Cooking time:** 20 minutes **Servings:** 6

## Ingredients:

- 1 pound and a half diced eggplant1 tbsp olive oil (extra virgin)
- Optional: 1 teaspoon garlic powderOptional: 1 teaspoon onion powder1 tablespoon of sumac.
- 2 tablespoons za'atar, 12 teaspoons lemon juice 2 bay leaves (optional).

## Directionsl:

1. In an air fryer, combine the eggplant cubes with the oil and seasonings of your choice: garlic powder, onion powder, sumac (or za'atar), lemon juice, and bay leaves. Cook at 370 degrees for 20 minutes.
2. Divide the mixture across plates and serve as a side dish. Enjoy!

Nutritional information: 172 calories, 4 grams of fat, 7 grams of fiber, 12 grams of carbohydrates, and 3 grams of protein.

# DELICIOUS AIR FRIED BROCCOLI

**Preparation time:** 10 minutes **Cooking time:** 20 minutes **Servings:** 4

## Ingredients:

- 1 tbsp (optional) duck fat
- 1 broccoli head (florets removed)
- 3 garlic cloves, peeled and minced.
- Lemon juice from 12 lemons
- 1 tbsp (optional) sesame seeds

## Directions:

1. Preheat the air fryer to 350°F, then add the duck fat and heat it up as well.
2. Add the broccoli, garlic, lemon juice, and sesame seeds to the pan and cook for 20 minutes, or until the broccoli is tender.
3. Divide the mixture among plates and serve with your meal as a side dish.Enjoy!

Nutrition: 132 calories, 3 grams of fat, 3 grams of fiber, 6 grams of carbohydrates, and 4 grams of protein.

# RICE AND SAUSAGE SIDE DISH

**Preparation time:** 10 minutes **Cooking time:** 20 minutes **Servings:** 4

## *Ingredients:*

- 2 cups of white rice that has already been boiled.
- 1 tablespoon of melted butter.
- Season with salt and black pepper to taste.
- 4 garlic cloves, peeled and minced.
- 1 pound of chopped pork sausage.
- 2 tbsp finely chopped grated carrot
- 3 tbsp (optional) grated cheddar cheese
- Shredded mozzarella cheese (about 2 tablespoons)

**Directions:**

1. Preheat your air fryer to 350°F. Add the butter and melt it, then add the garlic and stir for 2 minutes, or until it is lightly browned.
2. In a large mixing bowl, combine the sausage, salt, pepper, carrots, and rice and bake for ten minutes at 350 degrees F.
3. Toss in the cheddar and mozzarella until well combined, then divide among plates and serve as a side dish.
4. Enjoy!

Nutritional information 240 calories, 12 grams of fat, 5 grams of fiber, 20 grams of carbohydrates, and 13 grams of protein.

# SIMPLE POTATO CHIPS

**Preparation time:** 30 minutes **Cooking time:** 30 minutes **Servings:** 4

## *Ingredients:*

- 4 potatoes, cleaned and peeled into thin chips, then soaked in water for 30 minutes, drained, and patted dry.
- Season the flavor with salt.
- 1 tbsp olive oil (extra virgin)
- 2 tbsp rosemary, finely chopped

## Directions:

1. In a large mixing bowl, combine the potato chips with the salt and oil, tossing to coat completely. Place the chips in the air fryer basket and cook them at 330 degrees F for 30 minutes. 2.
2. Divide the mixture among the serving dishes and top with rosemary before serving as a side dish.
3. Enjoy!

Nutritional information: 200 calories, 4 grams of fat, 4 grams of fiber, 14 grams of carbohydrates, and 5 grams of protein.

# AIR FRIED CREAMY CABBAGE

**Preparation time:** 10 minutes **Cooking time:** 20 minute **Servings:** 4

## *Ingredients:*

- 1 head of green cabbage, finely chopped.
- 1 finely sliced small yellow onion
- Season with salt and black pepper to taste.
- finely diced bacon, sliced
- 1 gallon heavy whipping cream
- 2 tablespoons of cornstarch (optional)

## Directions:

1. In a large mixing bowl, combine the cabbage, bacon, and onion.
2. Combine cornstarch, cream, salt, and pepper in a large mixing bowl; stir well and pour over cabbage.
3. Toss, bake at 400°F for 20 minutes, divide among plates, and serve as a side dish.
4. Enjoy!

Nutritional values: 208 calories, 10 grams of fat, 3 grams of fiber, 16 grams of carbohydrates, and 5 grams of protein.

# TORTILLA CHIPS

**Preparation time:** 10 minutes **Cooking time:** 6 minutes **Servings:** 4

## *Ingredients:*

- makes eight corn tortillas that are cut into triangles.
- Season with salt and black pepper to taste.
- 1 tbsp olive oil (extra virgin)
- A pinch of garlic powder (optional).
- with a sprinkle of smoked paprika (sweet).

## Directions:

1. In a large mixing bowl, combine the tortilla chips with the oil, season with salt, pepper, garlic powder, and paprika, toss well, and then set them in the air fryer basket and cook for 6 minutes at 400 degrees F.
2. You can serve them as a side dish with a seafood meal.
3. Enjoy!

Nutritional information 53 calories, 1 gram of fat, 1 gram of fiber, 6 grams of carbohydrates, and 4 grams of protein.

# AIR FRYER SNACK AND APPETIZER RECIPES

# COCONUT CHICKEN BITES

**Preparation time:** 10 minutes **Cooking time:** 13 minutes **Servings:** 4

## Ingredients:

- 2 tablespoons of garlic powder (optional)
- Two quail eggs
- Season with salt and black pepper to taste.
- Panko bread crumbs (34 cup)
- 1/4 cup shredded coconut cooking spray
- 8 pieces of chicken tenders

## Directions:

1. In a large mixing bowl, whisk together the eggs, salt, pepper, and garlic powder until thoroughly combined.
2. In a separate bowl, combine the coconut and panko and whisk well.
3. Coat the chicken tenders in the egg mixture before dipping them in the coconut mixture.
4. Coat the chicken bits with cooking spray before placing them in the air fryer's basket and cooking them at 350 degrees F for 10 minutes until golden brown.
5. Arrange them on a serving platter and serve them to your guests as an appetizer.
6. Enjoy!

The following are the nutritional values: calories 252, fat 4, fiber 2, carbohydrates 14, protein 24.

# SHRIMP MUFFINS

**Preparation time:** 10 minutes **Cooking time:** 26 minutes **Servings:** 6

## Ingredients:

- 1 spaghetti squash, peeled and halved (about 1 pound).
- 2 tablespoons of mayonnaise (optional)
- 1 cup mozzarella cheese, shredded
- 8 ounces of raw shrimp, peeled, cooked, and chopped.
- 1 and 1/2 cups of panko breadcrumbs.
- 12 teaspoon (optional) parsley flakes1 peeled and minced garlic clove
- Season with salt and black pepper to taste. Using cooking spray

## Directions:

1. Cook the squash halves in the air fryer for 16 minutes at 350 degrees F.Remove it from the oven and set it aside to cool before scraping the flesh into a bowl.
2. Combine the salt, pepper, parsley flakes, panko, shrimp, mayonnaise, and mozzarella in a large mixing bowl. 3.
3. Lightly spray a muffin pan that will fit your air fryer with cooking spray, then divide the squash and shrimp mixture evenly among the cups.
4. Place the ingredients in the fryer and cook at 360°F for 10 minutes.
5. Arrange the muffins on a dish and give them as a snack to your guests.Enjoy!

Nutritional information: calories 60, fat 2 g, fiber 0.4 g, carbohydrates 4 g, protein 4 g.

# ZUCCHINI CHIPS

**Preparation time:** 10 minutes **Cooking time:** 1 hour **Servings:** 6

## *Ingredients:*

- 3 medium-sized zucchini, thinly sliced.
- Season with salt and black pepper to taste.
- 2 tbsp olive oil (extra-virgin)
- 2 teaspoons of vinegar (balsamic vinegar)

## Directions:

1. In a large mixing bowl, whisk together the oil, vinegar, salt, and pepper until thoroughly combined.
2. After adding the zucchini slices and tossing to coat well, cook at 200 degrees F for 1 hour in your air fryer.
3. As a snack, serve the zucchini chips chilled.
4. Enjoy!

Nutritional information 40 calories, 3 grams of fat, 7 grams of fiber, 3 grams of carbohydrates, and 7 grams of protein.

# HONEY PARTY WINGS

**Preparation time:** 1 hour and 10 minutes **Cooking time:** 12 minutes **Servings:**

8

## *Ingredients:*

- 16 chicken wings, each half-sized
- 2 tbsp. soy sauce (optional)
- Honey (about 2 tablespoons)
- Season with salt and black pepper to taste.
- Optional: 2 tbsp lime juice

**Directions:**

1. In a large mixing bowl, combine the chicken wings with the soy sauce, honey, salt, pepper, and lime juice, tossing well to coat. Refrigerate for 1 hour.
2. Place the chicken wings in the air fryer and cook them for 12 minutes at 360 degrees F, flipping them halfway through.
3. To serve, arrange the vegetables on a tray and serve them as an appetizer. Enjoy!

Nutritional information 211 calories, 4 grams of fat, 7 grams of fiber, 14 grams of carbohydrates, and 3 grams of protein.

# SALMON PARTY PATTIES

**Preparation time:** 10 minutes **Cooking time:** 22 minutes **Servings:** 4

## Ingredients:

- Boil 3 large russet potatoes until tender, drain, and mash.
- 1 large skinned and boned salmon fillet
- 2 teaspoons parsley, finely chopped
- 2 tbsp. finely chopped dill
- Season with salt and black pepper to taste.
- 1 quail (egg).
- Breadcrumbs (about 2 tablespoons) Using cooking spray

## Directions:

1. Formalized paraphrasePlace the salmon in the basket of your air fryer and cook for 10 minutes at 360 degrees Fahrenheit.
2. Transfer the salmon to a chopping board and allow it to cool before flaking it and placing it in a bowl.
3. 0 Combine the mashed potatoes, salt, pepper, dill, parsley, egg, and bread crumbs in a large mixing bowl and form 8 patties from the mixture.
4. Prepare your air fryer basket by spraying it with cooking oil and frying it at 360 degrees F for 12 minutes, flipping halfway through. Transfer the patties to a serving tray and serve as an appetiser.
5. Enjoy!

The following are the nutritional values: calories 231, fat 3, fiber 7, carbohydrates 14, protein 4.

# CRISPY RADISH CHIPS

**Preparation time:** 10 minutes **Cooking time:** 10 minutes **Servings:** 4

## Ingredients:

- Using cooking spray
- 15 radishes, peeled and sliced.
- Season with salt and black pepper to taste.
- 1 tablespoon chives, finely chopped

## Directions:

1. Place radish slices in the air fryer basket and spray them with cooking oil before seasoning them with salt and black pepper to taste. Cook for 10 minutes at 350°F, flipping halfway through.Transfer to serving bowls and garnish with chives.
2. Enjoy!

Nutritional information 80 calories, 1 gram of fat, 1 gram of fiber, 1 carbohydrate, 1 protein.

# CRAB STICKS

**Preparation time:** 10 minutes **Cooking time:** 12 minutes **Servings:** 4

## Ingredients:

- 10 crabsticks, each half-sized
- 2 tablespoons of sesame oil (optional)
- Cajun seasoning (about 2 teaspoons)

## Directions:

1. Place the crab sticks in a large mixing bowl and toss with the sesame oil and Cajun seasoning. Transfer the crab sticks to the basket of the air fryer and cook them at 350 degrees F for 12 minutes.
2. As an appetizer, arrange the ingredients on a tray and serve.
3. Enjoy!

110 calories, 1 gram of fiber, 4 carbohydrates, and 2 grams of protein

# CHICKPEAS SNACK

**Preparation time:** 10 minutes **Cooking time:** 10 minutes **Servings:** 4

## Ingredients:

- Drain 15 ounces of canned chickpeas before using them.
- 2 and 1/2 teaspoons of cumin seeds, finely ground
- 1 tbsp olive oil (extra virgin)
- 1 teaspoon (optional) smoked paprika
- Season with salt and black pepper to taste.

## Directions:

1. Toss chickpeas, oil, cumin, paprika, salt, and pepper together in a large mixing bowl.Place the chickpeas in a deep-fat fryer basket and cook at 390 degrees Fahrenheit for 10 minutes.
2. Divide the mixture into small dishes and serve as a snack.
3. Enjoy!

Nutritional information: calories 140, fat 1, fiber 6, carbohydrates 20, protein 6.

# SWEET POPCORN

**Preparation time:** 5 minutes **Cooking time:** 10 minutes **Servings:** 4

## *Ingredients:*

- 2 tablespoons of maize kernels (optional).
- 2 and 1/2 tablespoons melted butter
- 2 ounces of light brown sugar.

## Directions:

1. To begin, place corn kernels in the pan of your air fryer and cook at 400 degrees F for 6 minutes. Then transfer them to a baking sheet and spread them out evenly.
2. In a small saucepan, melt the butter until it is completely melted, then add the sugar and whisk until it is completely dissolved.
3. Pour in the popcorn and toss to coat, then remove from the heat and spread it out again on the tray.
4. Allow it to cool before dividing it into bowls and serving as a snack.
5. Enjoy!

Nutritional values: 70 calories, 0.2 fat grams, 0 fiber grams, 1 carbohydrate gram, 1 protein gram.

# APPLE CHIPS

**Preparation time:** 10 minutes **Cooking time:** 10 minutes **Servings:** 2

## Ingredients:

- 1 peeled and thinly sliced apple with a dash of seasoning
- 1 tsp to 1/2 tsp cinnamon powder
- 1 tablespoon of granulated sugar.

## Directions:

1. In a large mixing bowl, combine the apple slices with the salt, sugar, and cinnamon; toss well. Transfer them to the air fryer basket and cook for 10 minutes at 390 degrees F, flipping halfway through.
2. Arrange apple chips in serving bowls and serve as a light snack.
3. Enjoy!

Nutritional information: calories 70, fat zero, fiber four, carbohydrates three, protein one.

# CRISPY SHRIMP

**Preparation time:** 10 minutes **Cooking time:** 5 minutes **Servings:** 4

## Ingredients:

- 12 large shrimp that have been deveined and skinned
- 2 egg whites (optional).
- 1 cup (optional) shredded coconut
- Optional: 1 cup panko bread crumbs
- 1 cup of white flour (optional).
- Season with salt and black pepper to taste.

## Directions:

1. In a mixing bowl, combine the panko and coconut and stir well.
2. In a second bowl, combine the flour, salt, and pepper; in a third, beat the egg whites until stiff.
3. Dredge the shrimp in the flour, egg white mixture, and coconut, then set them all in the air fryer's basket. Cook for 10 minutes at 350 degrees F, flipping halfway through the cooking time.
4. Prepare it as an appetizer by arranging it on a dish and serving it immediately.
5. Enjoy!

Nutritional information: 140 calories, 4 grams of fat, 0 grams of fiber, 3 grams of carbohydrates, and 4 grams of protein.

# CRISPY FISH STICKS

**Preparation time:** 10 minutes **Cooking time:** 12 minutes **Servings:** 2

## Ingredients:

- 1 cup fresh parsley, coarsely chopped
- 4 tbsp extra virgin olive oil
- 1 lightly whisked egg
- Cut four boneless, skinless white fish filets into medium sticks after removing the bones and skin.
- Season with salt and black pepper to taste.

## Directions:

1. In a large mixing bowl, combine the bread crumbs and oil and toss thoroughly.
2. In a separate bowl, combine the egg, salt, and pepper until well combined.
3. Dip each fish stick in the egg and then in the bread crumb mixture, then set them in the air fryer's basket and cook for 12 minutes at 360 degrees Fahrenheit.
4. Arrange the fish sticks on a tray and serve them as an appetizer to your guests.
5. Enjoy!

Nutritional information: 160 calories, 3 grams of fat, 5 grams of fiber, 12 grams of carbohydrates, and 3 grams of protein.

# FISH NUGGETS

**Preparation time:** 10 minutes **Cooking time:** 12 minutes **Servings:** 4

## Ingredients:

- 28 ounces fish fillets (skinless and chopped into medium pieces)
- Season with salt and black pepper to taste.
- flour (approximately 5 tablespoons)
- 1 lightly whisked egg
- 5 tablespoons distilled water
- Panko bread crumbs (around 3 ounces)
- Garlic powder (about a tablespoon)
- 1-teaspoon hot and spicy smoked paprika
- 1 cup mayonnaise (homemade or store bought) 12 lemon juice
- 1 tsp. dried dill, 1 tsp. cooking spray

## Directions:

1. In a large mixing basin, whisk together the flour and the water until well combined.
2. Combine the egg, salt, and pepper in a mixing bowl.
3. In a second bowl, combine the panko, garlic powder, and paprika, stirring thoroughly.
4. Four: coat each piece of fish with a flour and egg mixture before dipping it in a panko mixture. Place the fish pieces in the air fryer basket and spray the fish pieces with cooking oil before cooking at 400 degrees F for 12 minutes.
5. In the meantime, whisk together the mayonnaise, dill, and lemon juice in a large mixing basin.
6. Prepare the fish nuggets on a tray and serve them with a side of dill mayo to accompany them.
7. Enjoy!

Nutritional values: 332 calories, 12 grams of fat, 6 grams of fiber, 17 grams of carbohydrates, and 15 grams of protein.

# CHICKEN BREAST ROLLS

**Preparation time:** 10 minutes **Cooking time:** 22 minutes **Servings:** 4

## Ingredients:

- 2 cups of baby spinach (optional)
- boneless and skinless chicken breasts (four breasts total)
- 1 cup sun-dried tomatoes, finely chopped
- Season with salt and black pepper to taste.
- 1 and a half teaspoons of Italian seasoning (optional). 4 pieces of mozzarella cheese.
- A little sprinkling of extra-virgin olive oil

## Directions:

1. Flatten the chicken breasts with a meat tenderizer. Divide the tomatoes, mozzarella, and spinach. Season with salt, pepper, and Italian seasoning. Then roll and seal the chicken breasts together.
2. Using your air fryer basket, sprinkle some oil over the vegetables and cook at 375 degrees F for 17 minutes, flipping halfway through the cooking time.
3. Prepare the chicken rolls as an appetizer by arranging them on a tray and serving them as an appetizer.
4. Enjoy!

Nutritional information 300 calories, 1 gram of fat, 4 grams of fiber, 7 grams of carbohydrates, and 10 grams of protein

# BEEF ROLL S

**Preparation time:** 10 minutes **Cooking time:** 14 minutes **Servings:** 4

## Ingredients:

- A two-pound beef steak that has been opened and flattened with a meat tenderizer.
- Season with salt and black pepper to taste.
- 1 cup (optional) baby spinach
- 1 red bell pepper, diced (after roasting)
- 6 slices of provolone cheese (optional).
- Pesto (about 3 tablespoons)

## Directions:

1. Place the flattened beef steak on a chopping board and spread pesto over the top. Sprinkle with cheese in a single layer and top with bell peppers, spinach, salt, and freshly ground pepper to taste.
2. Roll your steak and secure it with toothpicks before seasoning it again with salt and pepper.Place the roll in the air fryer's basket and cook at 400 degrees F for 14 minutes, flipping the roll halfway through.
3. After allowing them to cool, cut them into 2 inch mini rolls and place them on a tray before serving them as an appetizer.
4. Enjoy!

Nutritional information: calories 230, fat 1, fiber 3, carbohydrates 12, protein 10.

# AIR FRYER FISH AND SEAFOOD RECIPES

# TASTY AIR FRIED COD

**Preparation time:** 10 minutes **Cooking time:** 12 minutes **Servings:** 4

## *Ingredients:*

- 2 cod and 2 halibut
- Each weighed 7 ounces. A smidgeon of sesame oil is added.
- Season with salt and black pepper to taste.
- 1 c. distilled water
- 1 teaspoon (optional) dark soy sauce
- 4 tbsp. light soy sauce (optional)
- 1 tablespoon granulated sugar
- three tbsp extra-virgin olive oil4 pieces of ginger, thinly sliced.
- 3 spring onions, thinly sliced.
- 2 tablespoons finely chopped coriander leaves

## Directions:

1. Season the fish with salt and pepper, then sprinkle it with sesame oil and rub it in thoroughly. Set aside for 10 minutes.
2. Place the fish in your air fryer and cook it for 12 minutes at 356 degrees Fahrenheit.
3. In the meantime, bring water and dark and light soy sauce to a simmer in a pot over medium heat while stirring constantly. Remove from heat once the sauce has reached a simmering temperature.
4. Heat the olive oil in a saucepan over medium heat. Add the ginger and green onions, stirring constantly. Cook for a few minutes before removing from the heat.

5. Divide the fish among the dishes, garnish with ginger and green onions, pour in the soy sauce mixture, and sprinkle with coriander before serving immediately.
6. Enjoy!

Nutrition: 300 calories, 17 grams of fat, 8 grams of fiber, 20 grams of carbohydrates, and 22 grams of protein.

# DELICIOUS CATFISH

**Preparation time:** 10 minutes **Cooking time:** 20 minutes **Servings:** 4

## Ingredients:

- 4 catfish fillets (seafood)
- Season with salt and black pepper to taste.
- with a sprinkle of smoked paprika (sweet).
- 1 tablespoon parsley, finely chopped
- 1 tbsp lemon juice, freshly squeezed
- 1 tbsp olive oil (extra virgin)

## Directions:

1. Using salt, pepper, and paprika as seasonings, sprinkle oil over catfish fillets and rub them in thoroughly. Place the fish in an air fryer basket and cook at 400 degrees Fahrenheit for 20 minutes, flipping the fish after 10 minutes.
2. Before serving, arrange the fish on plates, drizzle with lemon juice, and garnish with parsley.
3. Enjoy!

Calorie count: 253, fat 6 grams, fiber 12 grams, carbohydrates 26 grams, protein 22 grams.

# BUTTERED SHRIMP SKEWERS

**Preparation time:** 10 minutes **Cooking time:** 6 minutes **Servings:** 2

## *Ingredients:*

- 8 shrimp that have been skinned and deveined
- 4 garlic cloves, peeled and minced.
- Season with salt and black pepper to taste.
- 8 green bell pepper slices, sliced thinly
- 1 tablespoon rosemary, finely chopped
- 1 tablespoon of melted butter (or margarine)

## Directions:

1. In a large mixing bowl, combine the shrimp with the garlic, butter, salt, pepper, rosemary, and bell pepper slices, tossing to coat the shrimp completely, and set it aside for 10 minutes.
2. Place 2 shrimp and 2 bell pepper slices on a skewer and continue the process with the remaining shrimp and bell pepper pieces.
3. Place all of the ingredients in the air fryer's basket and cook for 6 minutes at 360 degrees F.
4. Divide the mixture among the dishes and serve immediately.Enjoy!

Nutritional information: 140 calories, 1 gram of fat, 12 g fiber, 15 carbohydrates, 7 g protein.

# ASIAN SALMON

**Preparation time:** 1 hour **Cooking time:** 15 minutes **Servings:** 2

## Ingredients:

- 2 medium salmon fillets (about)
- light soy sauce (about 6 tablespoons).
- 3 tablespoons of mirin (optional).
- 1 tsp pure distilled water
- honey (about 6 teaspoons

**Directions:**

1. In a large mixing bowl, whisk together the soy sauce, honey, water, and mirin until well combined. Add the salmon and rub it in thoroughly before placing it in the refrigerator for 1 hour.
2. Place the salmon in the air fryer and cook at 360°F for 15 minutes, flipping after 7 minutes, or until cooked through.
3. Meanwhile, in a saucepan, bring the soy marinade to a simmer over medium heat, whisking constantly, for 2 minutes, then remove from heat.
4. Arrange the salmon on plates and drizzle them with the marinade before serving.
5. Enjoy!

Nutritional information 300 calories, 12 grams of fat, 8 grams of fiber, 13 grams of carbohydrates, and 24 grams of protein.

# C OD STEAKS WITH PLUM SAUCE

**Preparation time:** 10 minutes **Cooking time:** 20 minutes **Servings:** 2

## *Ingredients:*

- 2 large cod fillets.
- Season with salt and black pepper to taste.
- 1/2 teaspoon of garlic powder (optional).
- Optional: 1/2 teaspoon ginger powder
- 1/4 teaspoons of turmeric powder (optional)
- 1 tbsp (optional) plum sauceUsing cooking spray

## Directions:

1. Season the cod steaks with salt and pepper, spray them with cooking oil, sprinkle on the garlic powder, ginger powder, and turmeric powder, and rub everything together thoroughly.
2. Cook the cod steaks in the air fryer for 15 minutes at 360°F, flipping them after 7 minutes.
3. In a small saucepan, boil the plum sauce over medium heat, stirring constantly, for 2 minutes.
4. Arrange the fish steaks on plates, sprinkle the plum sauce over the top, and serve immediately.
5. Enjoy!

Nutritional information 250 calories, 7 grams of fat, 1 gram of fiber, 14 grams of carbohydrates, and 12 grams of protein.

# THYME AND PARSLEY SALMON

**Preparation time:** 10 minutes **Cooking time:** 15 minutes **Servings:** 4

## Ingredients:

- 4 salmon fillets, boneless, with the juice of one lemon
- 1 lemon (obligatory)
- 1 finely sliced small yellow onion
- 3 sliced tomatoes (optional).
- 4 springs of thyme.
- 4 parsley leaves and 4 parsley stems
- 3 tblsp. extra virgin olive oil (optional)
- Season with salt and black pepper to taste.

**Directions:**

1. In a pan that fits your air fryer, drizzle one tablespoon of oil, add a layer of tomatoes, salt and pepper, drizzle another tablespoon of oil, add the fish, season with salt and pepper, drizzle the rest of the oil, add thyme and parsley springs, onions, lemon juice, and season with salt and pepper, and place in the air fryer basket.Cook for 12 minutes at 360°F, shaking once during the cooking time.
2. Place everything on individual plates and serve right away.
3. Enjoy!

The following are the nutritional values: calories 242, fat 9, fiber 12, carbohydrates 20, protein 31.

# SWORDFISH AND MANGO SALSA

**Preparation time:** 10 minutes **Cooking time:** 6 minutes **Servings:** 2

## *Ingredients:*

- 2 swordfish steaks (medium-rare)
- Season with salt and black pepper to taste.
- A couple teaspoons of avocado oil
- 1 tablespoon cilantro, finely chopped
- 1 peeled and cut mango
- 1 pitted and halved avocado
- chopped after being peeled, a sprinkle of ground cumin
- A pinch of onion powder is used in this recipe. A pinch of garlic powder (optional).
- 1 orange, peeled and thinly sliced
- 1 tablespoon balsamic vinegar

**Directions:**

1. Cook for 6 minutes at 360 degrees F (turning halfway through) in your air fryer with half of the oil rubbed with salt, pepper, garlic powder, onion powder, and cumin.
2. Meanwhile, in a large mixing bowl, combine the avocado, mango, cilantro, balsamic vinegar, salt, pepper, and the remaining oil, stirring thoroughly.
3. Arrange the fish in individual dishes. Top with mango salsa and serve with orange slices on the side.
4. Enjoy!

Nutritional information 200 calories, 7 grams of fat, 2 grams of fiber, 14 grams of carbohydrates, 14 grams of protein.

# SALMON AND BLACKBERRY GLAZE

**Preparation time:** 10 minutes **Cooking time:** 33 minutes **Servings:** 4

## Ingredients:

- 1 c. distilled water
- Ginger, 1 inch piece, finely grated
- 1 tbsp freshly squeezed lemon juice
- 1 1/2 ounces fresh blackberries (optional)
- 1 tbsp olive oil (extra virgin)
- 1/4 cups of sugar (about)
- 4 medium salmon fillets (skinless), cooked in a skillet
- Season with salt and black pepper to taste.

## Directions:

1. In a pot over medium-high heat, bring the water to a boil for 4-5 minutes, then remove from heat and pour into a bowl before returning to the pan and combining with the sugar.2. In a separate bowl, combine the sugar and ginger.
2. Stir in the remaining ingredients and cook for 20 minutes on medium low heat.
3. Let the blackberry sauce cool before brushing it on the salmon and seasoning with salt and pepper.Drizzle olive oil all over the fish and press it in thoroughly.
4. Cook the fish in your prepared air fryer for 10 minutes at 350 degrees F, turning the fillets once during the cooking process.
5. Divide the mixture among the plates and sprinkle some of the remaining blackberry sauce over the top before serving.
6. Enjoy!

Nutritional information: 312 calories; 4 grams of fat; 9 grams of fiber; 19 grams of carbohydrates; and 14 grams of protein.

## AIR FRYER POULTRY RECIPES

# CREAMY COCONUT CHICKEN

**Preparation time:** 2 hours **Cooking time:** 25 minutes **Servings:** 4

## Ingredients:

- 4 large chicken thighs,
- About 5 tablespoons of turmeric powder
- 2 teaspoons ginger, freshly grated
- Season with salt and black pepper to taste.
- 1 cup (four teaspoons) coconut cream

## Directions:

1. In a large mixing bowl, whisk together the cream, turmeric, ginger, salt, and pepper. Add the chicken pieces and stir them thoroughly before setting them aside for 2 hours.
2. Place the chicken in the prepared air fryer and cook for 25 minutes at 370°F.Divide the chicken among plates and serve with a side salad on the side.
3. Enjoy!

Nutritional values: 300 calories, 4 grams of fat, 12 grams of fiber, 22 grams of carbohydrates, and 20 grams of protein.

# CHINESE CHICKEN WINGS

**Preparation time:** 2 hours **Cooking time:** 15 minutes **Servings:** 6

## Ingredients:

- 16 pieces of chicken wings
- Honey (about 2 tablespoons)
- 2 tbsp. soy sauce (optional)
- Season with salt and black pepper to taste.
- a quarter teaspoon freshly ground white pepper
- 3 tablespoons of lime juice (optional)

## Directions:

1. In a large mixing bowl, whisk together the honey, soy sauce, salt, black and white pepper, and lime juice until well combined. Add the chicken pieces and toss to coat, then refrigerate for 2 hours.
2. Place the chicken in the air fryer and cook for 6 minutes on each side at 370 degrees F. Then increase the heat to 400 degrees F and cook for 3 minutes more on each side.
3. Make sure to serve it hot.
4. Enjoy!

Nutritional information: calories 372, fat 9, fiber 10, carbohydrates 37, protein 24.

# HERBED CHICKEN

**Preparation time:** 30 minutes **Cooking time:** 40 minutes **Servings:** 4

## Ingredients:

- One entire chicken (about)
- Season with salt and black pepper to taste.
- Optional: 1 teaspoon garlic powder
- Optional: 1 teaspoon onion powder
- 12 teaspoons of thyme leaves (dry)
- 1 tsp rosemary (preferably dried)
- 1 tbsp lemon juice, freshly squeezed
- 2 tbsp olive oil (extra-virgin)

**Directions:**

1. Season the chicken with salt and pepper, then sprinkle it with thyme, rosemary, garlic powder, and onion powder before rubbing it with lemon juice and olive oil and setting it aside for 30 minutes. 2.
2. Place the chicken in the air fryer and cook it at 360 degrees F for 20 minutes on each side until done.
3. Take the chicken off the heat and set it aside to cool before carving and serving.
4. Enjoy!

Nutrition: 390 calories, 10 grams of fat, 5 grams of fiber, 22 grams of carbohydrates, and 20 grams of protein.

# MEXICAN CHICKEN

**Preparation time:** 10 minutes **Cooking time:** 20 minutes **Servings:** 4

## Ingredients:

- A 16-ounce jar of salsa verde
- 1 tbsp olive oil (extra virgin)
- Season with salt and black pepper to taste.
- 1 pound bone-in, skinless chicken breasts1 lb. rotisserie chicken
- 1 1/2 cups Monterey Jack cheese (grated)
- 1/4 cup cilantro, finely chopped
- Optional: 1 teaspoon garlic powder

## Directions:

1. Place salsa verde in a baking dish that is large enough to suit your air fryer. Season the chicken pieces with salt, pepper, and garlic powder before brushing them with olive oil and placing them on top of the salsa verde.
2. Place the ingredients in your air fryer and cook at 380°F for 20 minutes.
3. Sprinkle the cheese on top and continue to cook for another 2 minutes.
4. Divide the mixture among the plates and serve it immediately.Enjoy!

Nutritional information 340 calories, 18 grams of fat, 14 grams of fiber, 32 grams of carbohydrates, and 18 grams of protein.

# CHINESE DUCK LEGS

**Preparation time:** 10 minutes **Cooking time:** 36 minutes **Servings:** 2

## Ingredients:

- Two pieces of duck leg.
- 2 dried chile peppers, finely chopped.
- 1 tbsp olive oil (extra virgin)
- 2 sprigs star anise
- 1 bunch spring onions, finely chopped
- 4 pieces of ginger, thinly sliced.
- 1 tbsp (optional) oyster sauce
- 1 tbsp (optional) soy sauce
- Optional: 1 teaspoon sesame oil
- 14 ounces of pure water.
- 1 tbsp (optional) rice wine

## Directions:

1. Heat the oil in a large skillet over medium-high heat, then add the chilies, star anise, sesame oil, rice wine, ginger, oyster sauce, soy sauce, and water, stirring constantly, and cook for 6 minutes until the chilies are soft. 2.
2. Toss in the spring onions and duck legs to coat, then transfer to an air fryer-safe pan and cook at 370°F for 30 minutes, or until the duck legs are cooked through.
3. Distribute the mixture among the plates and serve.
4. Enjoy!

Nutritional information 300 calories, 12 grams of fat, 12 grams of fiber, 26 grams of carbohydrates, and 18 grams of protein.

# DUCK AND PLUM SAUCE

**Preparation time:** 10 minutes **Cooking time:** 32 minutes **Servings:** 2

## *Ingredients:*

- 2 duck breasts (separately)
- 1 tablespoon of melted butter (or margarine)
- 1 star anise (approximately)
- 1 tbsp olive oil (extra virgin)
- 1 peeled and chopped shallot
- 9 ounces of red plums, peeled and stoned, cut into thin wedges.
- 1 cup sugar (approximately 2 teaspoons)
- 2 tblsp. of dry red wine.
- Optional: 1 cup beef stock

**Directions:**

1. Prepare the shallot by heating it in a skillet with olive oil over medium heat until it begins to soften, about 5 minutes.
2. Combine the sugar and plums in a mixing bowl and stir until the sugar is completely dissolved.
3. Cook for 15 minutes on low heat, stirring constantly, before removing from heat and keeping warm for now.
4. Score the duck breasts, season them with salt and pepper, and rub them with melted butter. Transfer the duck breasts to a heat-proof dish that fits your air fryer, add the star anise and the plum sauce, and cook at 360 degrees F for 12 minutes.
5. Arrange all of the ingredients on individual plates and serve.
6. Enjoy!

Nutritional information: 400 calories, 25 grams of fat, 12 grams of fiber, 29 grams of carbohydrates, and 44 grams of protein.

# CHICKEN THIGHS AND APPLE MIX

**Preparation time:** 12 hours **Cooking time:** 30 minutes **Servings:** 4

## *Ingredients:*

- 8 bone-in and skin-on chicken thighs (bones removed).
- Season with salt and black pepper to taste.
- Apple cider vinegar (about 1 tablespoon)
- 3 tablespoons finely diced onion
- 1 tbsp ginger, finely grated
- 1/2 teaspoons of thyme leaves (dry)
- Cut 3 apples into quarters once they have been cored.
- one-quarter cup apple juice
- 1/2 cup pure maple syrup

### Directions:

1. In a large mixing bowl, combine the chicken, salt, pepper, vinegar, onion, ginger, thyme, apple juice, and maple syrup; toss well to combine. Refrigerate for 12 hours with the lid on.
2. After transferring the entire mixture to a baking dish that fits your air fryer, cook at 350 degrees F for 30 minutes.
3. Divide the mixture among the plates and serve immediately.
4. Enjoy!

Nutritional information: 314 calories; 8 grams of fat; 11 grams of fiber; 34 grams of carbohydrates; and 22 grams of protein.

# CHICKEN AND LENTILS CASSEROLE

**Preparation time:** 10 minutes **Cooking time:** 1 hour **Servings:** 8

## Ingredients:

- Green lentils (about 1 to 1/2 cups)
- 3 quarts of chicken broth.
- Chicken breasts (skinless, boneless, diced) weighing 2 pounds
- Season with salt and cayenne pepper to taste.
- Spray cooking oil with cumin (three teaspoons)
- 5 garlic cloves, peeled and minced.
- 1 finely sliced small yellow onion
- 2 red bell peppers, peeled and diced.
- 14 ounces of canned tomatoes, finely minced
- 2 cup boiled corn
- 2 cups (optional) shredded Cheddar cheese
- 2 teaspoons jalapeo pepper, finely chopped
- Garlic powder (about a tablespoon)
- 1 cup cilantro, finely chopped

## Directions:

1. In a large pot, bring the stock to a boil over medium heat while stirring in the lentils. Cover and cook for 35 minutes until the lentils are tender.
2. In the meantime, spray the chicken pieces with cooking spray and season them with salt, cayenne pepper, and 1 teaspoon cumin before placing them in the air fryer's basket and cooking for 6 minutes at 370 degrees, rotating them half way through. 3.
3. Add the bell peppers, garlic, tomatoes, onion, salt, cayenne pepper, and 1 teaspoon cumin to the chicken in a

heatproof dish that fits your air fryer. 4. Cook for 10 minutes on high.

4. Drain the lentils and add them to the chicken mixture as well as the tomatoes.
5. Combine the jalapeno pepper, garlic powder, the remaining cumin, the corn, half of the cheese, and half of the cilantro in a large mixing bowl. Place the mixture in the air fryer and cook at 320 degrees F for 25 minutes until the cheese is melted.
6. Sprinkle the remaining cheese and cilantro on top, then divide the chicken casserole among the dishes and serve immediately.
7. Enjoy!

Nutritional information: 344 calories, 11 grams of fat, 12 grams of fiber, 22 grams of carbohydrates, and 33 grams of protein.

# DUCK AND VEGGIES

**Preparation time:** 10 minutes **Cooking time:** 20 minutes **Servings:** 8

## Ingredients:

- 1 duck breast, peeled and cut into medium-sized pieces
- 3 peeled and cut cucumbers
- (white wine) (three tablespoons)
- 2 carrots, peeled and sliced.
- 1 cup (optional) chicken stock
- 1 tiny piece of grated ginger (about 1 teaspoon)
- Season with salt and black pepper to taste.

## Directions:

1. In a pan that will accommodate your air fryer, combine the duck pieces with the cucumbers, the white wine, and the carrots. Add the ginger and the stock and season with salt and pepper. 2. Place the pan in your air fryer and cook for 20 minutes at 370°F.
2. Arrange all of the ingredients on individual plates and serve.
3. Enjoy!

Nutritional information: 200 calories, 10 grams of fat, 8 grams of fiber, 20 grams of carbohydrates, and 22 grams of protein.

**Preparation time:** 10 minutes **Cooking time:** 12 minutes **Servings:** 2

## Ingredients:

- Boneless chicken breasts weigh 1/2 pound.
- 1 small peeled and diced yellow onion
- 2 teaspoons garlic, finely minced
- A teaspoon of freshly grated ginger.
- a pinch of finely chopped allspice
- Four water chestnut slivers (four tablespoons)
- 2 tbsp. soy sauce (optional)
- Chicken stock (about 2 teaspoons)
- 2 teaspoons of vinegar (balsamic vinegar)
- 2 tortillas for slicing and serving.

**Directions:**

1. Cook at 360°F for 12 minutes in a pan that fits your air fryer. 1. In a large mixing bowl, combine the chicken meat with the onion and garlic and stir until well combined. 2. Place in your air fryer and cook for 12 minutes at 360°F.
2. Arrange all of the ingredients on individual plates and serve.

Nutritional information: 301 calories, 12 grams of fat, 7 grams of fiber, 24 grams of carbohydrates, and 12 grams of protein.

# DUCK AND CHERRIES

**Preparation time:** 10 minutes **Cooking time:** 20 minutes **Servings:** 4

## *Ingredients:*

- (approximately) 1/2 cup sugar
- 1/4 cup of honey.
- A third cup of balsamic vinegar
- 1 teaspoon garlic, finely minced
- 1 tbsp ginger, freshly grated1 tsp cumin, freshly ground
- ground to a paste (12 teaspoons)
- 1 to 12 teaspoons cinnamon powder
- 4 sage leaves, finely minced.
- 1 finely chopped jalapeno
- 2 cups rhubarb, thinly sliced
- 1/2 cup finely sliced yellow onion
- 2 cups of pitted cherries (optional)
- 4 boneless duck breasts with the skin on and scored
- Season with salt and black pepper to taste.

## Directions:

1. Season the duck breast with salt and pepper before placing it in the air fryer for 5 minutes on each side at 350°F.
2. Cook for 10 minutes while keeping an eye on the temperature of the pan. 2. In a medium-sized pan over medium heat, heat the sugar and honey until the sugar is dissolved, then add the vinegar and the rest of the ingredients (garlic, ginger, cumin, clove, cinnamon, sage), stirring constantly until the sugar is completely dissolved.
3. Add the duck breasts and stir well before dividing everything between plates and serving it. Enjoy!

Nutritional information: calories 456, fat 13 (fiber 4), carbohydrates 64, protein 31.

# MARINATED DUCK BREASTS

**Preparation time:** 1 day **Cooking time:** 15 minutes
**Servings:** 2

## Ingredients:

- 2 duck breasts (separately)
- 1 c. dry white wine
- Optional: 1/4 cup soy sauce
- 2 garlic cloves, peeled and minced.
- tarragon springs (six)
- Season with salt and black pepper to taste.
- 1 tablespoon of melted butter.
- 1/4-cup sherry wine (optional)

## Directions:

1. Toss the duck breasts with the white wine, soy sauce, garlic, tarragon, salt, and pepper in a large mixing basin and store in the refrigerator for up to one day.
2. Preheat the air fryer to 350°F and cook the duck breasts for 10 minutes, flipping halfway through the cooking time.
3. In the meantime, pour the marinade into a saucepan and bring it to a simmer over medium heat while stirring constantly. Cook for 5 minutes until the sauce has reduced by half and then remove it from the heat.
4. Arrange the duck breasts on plates and sprinkle the sauce over them before serving. Enjoy!

Nutritional information: 475 calories, 12 grams of fat, 3 grams of fiber, 10 grams of carbohydrates, and 48 grams of protein.

# CHICKEN AND RADISH MIX

**Preparation time:** 10 minutes **Cooking time:** 30 minutes **Servings:** 4

## *Ingredients:*

- 4 bone-in chicken breasts, skin-on
- Season with salt and black pepper to taste.
- 1 tbsp olive oil (extra virgin)
- 1 cup (optional) chicken stock
- 6 radishes, peeled and halved.
- 1 tablespoon table sugar
- 3 carrots, thinly sliced into sticks.
- 2 tbsp chives, finely chopped

## Directions:

1. Preheat a pan that will fit your air fryer over medium heat, then add the stock, carrots, sugar, and radishes, stirring gently to combine. Reduce the heat to medium, partially cover the pot, and simmer for 20 minutes.
2. Season the chicken breasts with salt and pepper before placing them in the air fryer for 4 minutes at 350 degrees F.
3. Toss the chicken with the radish mixture before placing everything in the air fryer and cooking for another 4 minutes before dividing amongst plates and serving.
4. Enjoy!

Nutritional information: 237 calories, 10 grams of fat, 4 grams of fiber, 19 grams of carbohydrates, and 29 grams of protein.

# CONCLUSION

Air frying has become one of the most popular cooking methods in recent years, and air fryers have evolved into some of the most incredible kitchen appliances.

Air fryers allow you to prepare nutritious and delicious meals in a short amount of time. Making exceptional recipes for yourself and your family does not necessitate becoming a culinary genius.

All you need is an air fryer and this fantastic air fryer cookbook to get started.

You will soon be able to prepare the most delectable foods, and you will be able to surprise everyone around you with your home-cooked meals!

Just put your faith in us! Get your hands on an air fryer and this selection of essential air fryer recipes to get started on your new cooking adventure!

Have a good time!

Made in United States
Troutdale, OR
11/21/2024

25133336R00075